Stories of the Victorian Writers

Stories of the Victorian Writers

By Mrs Hugh Walker

Author of *Outlines of Victorian Literature,*
A Book of Victorian Poetry
and Prose

Cambridge
at the University Press
1922

CAMBRIDGE
UNIVERSITY PRESS

University Printing House, Cambridge CB2 8BS, United Kingdom

Cambridge University Press is part of the University of Cambridge.

It furthers the University's mission by disseminating knowledge in the pursuit of
education, learning and research at the highest international levels of excellence.

www.cambridge.org
Information on this title: www.cambridge.org/9781107544567

First published 1922
First paperback edition 2015

A catalogue record for this publication is available from the British Library

ISBN 978-1-107-54456-7 Paperback

PREFACE

THE aim of this little volume is to induce those readers—whether young or old—who are not already familiar with the great Victorians to seek at least a bowing acquaintance with them and their works. With this end in view I have introduced into the narrative as many vivid and amusing stories as I could find, but anecdotes of doubtful authenticity have been avoided.

I desire to offer my sincere thanks to Mr S. C. Roberts, who has patiently and skilfully revised my MS.

For the anecdotes embodied in the book I am indebted to such biographies as: J. H. Froude, *Thomas Carlyle*; Sir G. O. Trevelyan, *Life of Macaulay*; Sir E. T. Cook, *Life of Ruskin*; W. G. Collingwood, *Life and Work of Ruskin*; Lord Tennyson, *Alfred, Lord Tennyson*; Arthur Waugh, *Alfred, Lord Tennyson*; W. H. Griffin and H. C. Minchin, *Life of Robert Browning*; J. W. Cross, *George Eliot's Life*; J. Forster, *Life of Charles Dickens*; E. C. Gaskell, *Life of Charlotte Brontë*.

I have also to thank Sir William Robertson Nicoll for many valuable suggestions, and I owe much to the British Museum officials who put at my command innumerable articles, magazines and unpublished letters.

Last, though not least, I am indebted to that comprehensive work by my husband, *The Literature of the Victorian Era*. I owe everything to him and to him I dedicate this little volume.

J. WALKER.

Lampeter,
   21 *June*, 1922.

CONTENTS

ILLUSTRATIONS

THOMAS CARLYLE

IN the Scottish lowlands, a part of the country which in the old days of strife between England and Scotland was the scene of much hardship and border warfare, there is a little, straggling, one-street village called Ecclefechan. Here, in 1795, Thomas Carlyle was born in a house which his father, a stone-mason, had built with his own hands. In later years Carlyle wrote in love and admiration of his father's work:

Nothing that he undertook to do but he did it faithfully and like a true man. I shall look on the houses he built with a certain proud interest. They stand firm and sound to the heart all over his little district....Am not I also the humble James Carlyle's work? I owe him much more than existence, I owe him a noble inspiring example.

The Carlyles' house stood near the middle of the village street, and down the side of the street ran a stream in which Carlyle paddled barefooted with the ducks as a boy. To-day the ducks still paddle in the little burn, while Carlyle sleeps in the grave-yard on the other side of his old home, his feet almost touching the kitchen wall.

In his childhood Carlyle had a violent temper, and his earliest memory was of himself at the age of two: "I had broken my little brown stool, by madly throwing it at my brother, and felt, for per-haps the first time, the united pangs of loss and remorse." He could remember, too, how, in his fifth year, his father taught him "arithmetical things, especially how to divide," and how later, on a Whitsuntide morning, 1805, he was taken down to Annan Academy, six miles away. The story of this journey is told in Carlyle's famous book *Sartor Resartus*, a curious title which means "the cobbler mended."

Well do I still remember (he says) the red sunny Whitsuntide morning, when, trotting full of hope by the side of Father Andreas, I entered the main street of the place [Annan], and saw its steeple-clock (then striking eight), and *Schuldthurm* (Jail), and the aproned, or disaproned Burghers moving-in to breakfast: a little dog, in mad terror was rushing past; for some human imps had tied a tin-kettle to its tail....[My school-fellows] were Boys, mostly rude Boys, and obeyed the impulse of rude Nature, which bids the deer-herd fall upon any stricken hart, the duck-flock put to death any broken-winged brother or sister, and on all hands the strong tyrannise over the weak.

Carlyle had to the end of his life a painful memory of these cruel schoolfellows; and his mother, quite innocently, added to her son's suffering. She felt afraid of Tom's sharp temper and, to save him from himself, made him promise never to return a blow. For some time he kept the promise he gave her, but in the end he could restrain himself no longer, and turned upon the biggest bully in the school and kicked him. There was a fight and Tom was beaten, but not until he had left his mark upon the enemy. After this Carlyle was left alone, but he never forgot the cruel usage he had borne at the Annan Academy, and he made but few friends among his schoolfellows.

In his fourteenth year Carlyle began life as a student of the University of Edinburgh. In the early days of last century the Dumfriesshire lads who were going to college set out on foot, having no money to pay for the coach-ride of seventy miles. On reaching Edinburgh they entered their names as students and found their own lodgings. The landladies let them the room and kept it clean, but the boys had to cook for themselves and otherwise see after their small needs. Carriers brought them oatmeal and other food from home and took back their soiled linen to be washed and mended.

The memory of that frosty November morning when Carlyle set out for his walk to Edinburgh never faded, and he often told how his father and mother started with him and kept him company for a little way. Like most Scottish parents they hoped to have a son able " to wag his head in the pulpit," and no sacrifice was too great to help their boy to reach this high calling. Their grief was, therefore, very deep when they discovered, towards the end of his college life, that he did not wish to be a minister.

When Carlyle left Edinburgh (which he called "the worst of all hitherto discovered universities") the only profession open to him was teaching, and for that he had little liking or patience. It was Edward Irving who found him his first post as master in Kirkcaldy in Fifeshire, where he himself was a master in a neighbouring school. The two young men became great friends, and one vacation Irving took Carlyle with him on a visit to Haddington. There he introduced him to Dr and Mrs Welsh, and to their beautiful daughter, Jane, who had been Irving's pupil. It was this girl who afterwards became Carlyle's wife.

As a little girl, Jane Welsh was an eager scholar, reading Latin when she was seven. When she began to read Virgil, she became ashamed of playing with dolls, so on her tenth birthday she "built a funeral pile of lead pencils and sticks of cinnamon, and poured some sort of perfume over all....She then recited the speech of Dido, stabbed her doll, and let out all the sawdust; after which she consumed her to ashes, and then burst into a passion of tears."

One of her most intimate friends said of her: "The first thing I ever heard of her was that she dressed well—an excellent gift for a woman," and there is no doubt that Jeannie Welsh had a wonderful talent for making pretty things. Once, when her mother wanted a specially fine, but not expensive, dress for a party, Jeannie offered to gather ivy trails and mosses of different sorts. These she draped round her mother's dress, and the effect was so good that everyone mistook them for expensive French trimmings.

The Welsh family claimed descent from John Knox, the sixteenth-century reformer, to whom Scotland owes the schools which gave her boys and girls a better education than the children of any other land. Thus Carlyle's young wife brought him not only beauty and wit, but noble lineage, as well as a dowry which included the mountain farm of Craigenputtock, which became for six years the home of the young couple.

Before they were married, when Carlyle proposed that they should start housekeeping in this desolate house, she refused even to consider the idea, and said: "Think of some more promising plan than farming the most barren spot in the county of Dumfriesshire. What a thing that would be to be sure! You and I keeping house at Craigenputtock; I would as soon think of building myself a nest on the Bass rock....I could not spend a month at it with an angel."

However, Carlyle was determined to go there, and for six years this lonely moorland house was her home. They began their married life in Edinburgh, but Carlyle could not work in a city; he longed for solitude, and Craigenputtock, thirty miles distant from Dumfries, the nearest town, offered him the peace he felt he must have. Four months after they had settled there, he wrote of it as "the devil's own den." But in the end the high mountain air and the solitude proved it to be the right place for Carlyle; its fitness for his wife is less certain.

In this far-away house Mrs Carlyle had to apply her genius to learning how to keep house, to clean and to cook. The first time she tried to make a pudding, she went into the kitchen and locked the door. It was to be made of suet, and with great thought and care she prepared her materials and mixed them. To her joy it turned out to be very good. Her first bread-making was another adventure. "I can remember very well," writes Carlyle, "her coming in to me, late at night (eleven or so), with her first loaf, looking mere triumph and quizzical gaiety: 'See!' The loaf was excellent, only the crust a little burnt....From that hour we never wanted excellent bread."

One of the great worries of Carlyle's life was indigestion; and if Mrs Carlyle had not devoted her life and gifts to keeping him strong and healthy as far as he could be so, Carlyle could never have done the great work he accomplished. From the beginning of her married life she made up her mind that her husband should never be forced to write for money, but only when he felt he had in his heart a message for the world. By careful economy of food and clothes she managed so well that no one ever guessed how poor they really were.

It was Carlyle himself who first let the world know of their poverty. In 1833 he wrote: "It is now some three and twenty months since I have earned one penny by the craft of literature." He was then thirty-eight years old and he had not wasted an hour of his working life, yet all that he had was £200, and with that small purse he and his wife left Craigenputtock and moved to Cheyne Row, Chelsea, to try their fortune in London.

During the six years of life on the farm Carlyle had never laid down his pen. *The Diamond Necklace* and many short pieces had been written. That wonderful history of his own mind, *Sartor Resartus*, was finished. *The French Revolution* also was planned and brooded over amongst the lonely Scottish hills. A tragedy is attached to this famous book: the manuscript of the first volume was lent to his friend John Stuart Mill to read, and a careless housemaid used the precious sheets to light a fire. This was a heart-breaking incident to Carlyle, for though he spent his life in writing books, he found it no easy task. He tells us that "after two weeks of blotching and bloring he had been able to write only two clean pages."

Meanwhile the sky looked very black for the Carlyles. No one could be found willing to print *Sartor Resartus*. And when at length the editor of *Fraser's Magazine* gave it a place in its pages, many of the readers of the journal refused to continue subscribing unless it was withdrawn.

However, the longest lane has its turning, and three years later Carlyle won his place amongst the great writers of his time. In 1837 he finished *The French Revolution*. When it was done, he flung the manuscript into his wife's lap, saying: "I know not whether this book is worth anything, nor what the world will do with it, or misdo, or entirely forbear to do, as is likeliest; but this I could tell the world: You have not had for a hundred years any book that comes more direct and flamingly from the heart of a living man." The book received recognition at once and Carlyle from that time stood in the front rank of English men of letters.

This sudden jump to fame did not, however,

immediately bring him a large sum of money, and
he began to form plans to emigrate to America
where, he was told, he would be well paid as a lecturer. Luckily for Britain this project was stopped.
It was arranged, instead, that he should deliver
lectures in London, and by them he earned the
money he needed.

The last course of lectures dealt with the subject
of heroes and great men. Later he put them into
a book called *Heroes and Hero-Worship*. Carlyle
always worshipped the great men: "Great men,"
he says, "are the inspired texts of that divine Book
of Revelations, whereof a chapter is completed
from epoch to epoch, and by some named History."
In his essay upon Scott he has enlarged still further
upon this favourite idea and says: "No heroic poem
in the world but is at bottom a biography, the life
of a man"; and he adds conversely, "there is no
life of a man, faithfully recorded, but is a heroic
poem of its sort, rhymed or unrhymed." In two of
his greatest books, *Cromwell* and *Frederick the Great*,
he tries to set forth his belief in the influence of the
lives of great men upon the history of the world
and upon the fortunes of those who live in it.

Carlyle lived to be a very old man; and perhaps
the proudest moment in his long life was when, in
1865, his old university of Edinburgh made him
its Lord Rector. This hour of glory was also the
saddest, for as he turned away from the speeches
and pageants of the ceremony of installation, he
learnt that his wife had been found dead in her
carriage driving home to Chelsea, from Hyde Park.

She had stopped her carriage to let out her little dog for a run, and her death was hastened by the horror of seeing it run over by a passing wheel. The animal escaped injury, but the heart of its mistress ceased to beat. With her life that of Carlyle practically ended also. He lived for fifteen years longer, but his hand trembled so that he could not write, and he found it impossible to dictate his thoughts to a secretary.

He lived on in Chelsea, much in the company of his biographer, J. A. Froude. They walked together daily, and Carlyle, in a mackintosh, and wearing a strange, broad-brimmed hat, let the weather do its worst. Often he took a bus to Hyde Park, and the conductors knew him well. A stranger once asked one of them who the old fellow was with the "queer hat."

"Queer 'at," answered the driver; "ay, he may wear a queer 'at, but what would you give for the 'ed-piece that's inside of it?"

When he was offered a title by Queen Victoria, which he refused, a bus-conductor remarked to Froude:

"Fine old gentleman that...we thinks a deal on him down in Chelsea."

"Yes," said Froude, "and the Queen thinks a deal on him too, for she offered to make him a Grand Cross."

"Very proper of she to think of it," answered the conductor, "and more proper of he to have nothing to do with it. 'Tisn't that as can do honour to the likes of he."

Of the long list of books which Carlyle wrote (nearly forty volumes in all) some are still widely read, others only by students of history and literature, for he wrote in a style that often makes it difficult to understand his thoughts. *Heroes and Hero-Worship* is one of the easier books to read and shows how passionately Carlyle believed that we must look to great men—whether kings, or poets, or priests, or soldiers—to govern the world, since the divine fire burns more brightly in them than in the rest.

In other ways, too, Carlyle stood out amongst the men of his time: he saw that it was not good for England that she should aim only at successful trading and manufacture; that cheap food and votes for everyone would not necessarily make a perfect nation; and while he insisted that every man must work, he insisted also that every man was a "Breath of God" and that the "lamp of his soul" should not be allowed to go out. "That there should one Man die ignorant, who had capacity for knowledge, this I call a tragedy."

THOMAS BABINGTON MACAULAY

IT is fitting that the birthday of the great English historian, Macaulay, should have been St Crispin's day, the anniversary of the battle of Agincourt. Thomas Babington Macaulay was born on October 25, 1800, in an ancient house, called Rothley Temple; and the dark, oak-panelled room was a birthplace well suited to the man who was to delight the world with his romantic histories. For Macaulay was later to change what had been for

THOMAS CARLYLE

most people a dry study into something which was as fascinating to read as a story book. He did not himself belong to an aristocratic family, but his aunt had married the squire of Rothley Temple, and at the time of his birth his mother was a guest in her brother-in-law's house.

The real playground of his babyhood was in the heart of the city of London, in Drapers' Gardens, about a hundred yards from the Stock Exchange. To these so-called gardens his nurse used to take him for fresh air, and many years later it still continued to be one of Macaulay's favourite haunts.

He remembered as a child looking out of the nursery window at the black smoke pouring out of a neighbouring chimney, and deeply paining his father, Zachary Macaulay, by asking him if it was hell; for the Macaulays were sprung from a generation or two of Scottish ministers who preached sternly of the hell that was in store for sinners.

We may well marvel how these ill-paid ministers brought up their large families. They fed them chiefly upon porridge, and when Carlyle looked at the round, fat face of Lord Macaulay, after he had become famous, he said: "Well, anyone can see that you are a good honest fellow, made out of oatmeal." Whatever they were made of, it is certain that all the members of the Macaulay family tried to leave the world a better place than they had found it, and it was Zachary Macaulay who, perhaps, more than any other Englishman, helped to carry through the House of Commons the bill which gave freedom to the slaves. Up to that time the poor creatures had been treated as soulless animals, bred like cattle and offered for sale in the open markets. Zachary Macaulay had been in the heart of the trade, for he was manager of a sugar plantation in Jamaica, and had he so chosen, he could have become a very rich man; but he chose rather to give up his life to secure the liberty of the poor negroes, giving up a well-paid post and placing all his knowledge at the disposal of the reformers.

He found in his wife, Miss Mills of Bristol, a warm helper in this great work. She belonged to the Society of Friends and amongst her acquaintances was Miss Hannah More, to whom many of Tom's early letters were written. She tells us, laughingly, of her first meeting with her favourite. Calling one day upon his parents, a fair-haired boy of four opened the door and told her that they were both out; but "Come in," he urgently begged, "and I will bring you a glass of old spirits." Miss More, a strict teetotaller, was somewhat shocked by the suggestion, and asked him what he knew about old spirits, and he answered that Robinson Crusoe often had some.

It was about the same time that Tom went with his father to visit Lady Waldegrave, at Strawberry Hill. He was finely dressed in a green coat, red collar and cuffs, a frill at the neck and white trousers. At luncheon a servant spilt some hot coffee over the little boy's legs. The hostess, much troubled, began to comfort him, but he astonished her by looking calmly up into her face and saying, "Thank you, madam, the agony is abated."

This sounds very conceited and silly, but Tom was really a very simple little boy. There were now plenty of brothers and sisters in the home, and very happy times they had playing upon Clapham Common, where their father had taken a house. The gravel pits, gorse bushes, and ponds scattered over the common became in his imaginative mind battle fields, robbers' caves, and wild deserts where men were lost, and children found. It is interesting to notice that even at that early age he showed strict notions about the Law, notions appropriate to one who was later to reform the Penal code for the government of India. He held severe views about the sacredness of his own little plot of garden which he had marked off from the big garden with rows of old oyster-shells. These a servant once threw away, and when he saw what she had done, he marched into the drawing-room where his mother had visitors, and in a loud voice said: "Cursed be Sally: for it is written, 'Cursed is he that removeth his neighbour's landmark.'"

He could not have been more than eight when he took it into his head to write a history of the world from the creation to his own day, but he filled so much paper that it is supposed that his mother cut off supplies. It ends abruptly with Oliver Cromwell, whom the small historian calls "an unjust man." Someone introduced him to Scott's *Lay of the Last Minstrel* and *Marmion*, and they pleased him so much that he learnt them both by heart. But nearly everything he read stayed in his memory and when he was quite old he could repeat the most out-of-the-way things, not only verses but such dry details as lists of the names of the men who had in the past been senior wranglers of the University of Cambridge.

When Tom was thirteen he was sent to a small school at Little Shelford, near Cambridge, where only twelve boys could be taken. There was no football or cricket at the school and the only outside interest was a walk into Cambridge, or the entertainment of the masters or tutors of the colleges by their own headmaster On Sundays there were long sermons to be listened to and then written out. "After tea," Tom wrote to his father, "we write out the sermon. I cannot help thinking that Mr Preston [the headmaster] uses all imaginable means to make us forget it, for he gives us a glass of wine each on Sunday, and on Sunday only, the very day when we want to have all our faculties awake; and some do literally go to sleep during the sermon, and look rather silly when they wake. I, however, have not fallen into this disaster."

His wonderful memory was to last all through his life, and he used to say that if some miracle came to sweep away all the copies of Milton's *Paradise Lost* or *The Pilgrim's Progress* from the world, he would be able to write out both again from memory. He could read, too, faster than anyone else, yet he never forgot what he had once seen in print, even though it were a trashy novel.

It was in 1818 that Macaulay entered Trinity College, Cambridge, and through life his College and his home held the two first places in his affections. The honour he most valued after he left Cambridge was the Fellowship which gave him the right to live again in a college room, to breakfast on commons, and to dine in hall at the high table beneath the portraits of Newton and Bacon. As a student he gained the Chancellor's medal for English verse, but mathematics, then compulsory for all honours men, were always a burden to him, and when the tripos examination list came out it was found that he had been "gulfed"—that is, his name was not to be found amongst those who had taken honours. Two years later, however, he was more than consoled by being made a Fellow of Trinity.

About the age of twenty-five he began to write, for *The Edinburgh Review*, the famous *Essays* which were later to bring him fame; he also worked for a short time as a barrister, but he was not attracted by the law, and preferred to sit in the gallery of the House of Commons, listening to the debates upon the slave question. When opportunity offered he helped his father by speaking in public in favour of the great cause.

One of his friends thus described his appearance at this time: "A short, manly figure, marvellously upright, with a bad neckcloth, and one hand in his waistcoat pocket." From his nephew Trevelyan, who afterwards wrote his life, we learn that he dressed badly, though his coats were always good, and he had scores of embroidered waistcoats. He was almost useless with his hands and had dozens of pairs of gloves into which he never got his fingers

more than halfway. When his rooms were turned
out after he had left for India, they were found to
be almost full of strops hacked into strips, and of
innumerable razors. Once, after an accident to his
hand, he sent for a barber. After the man had
finished, Macaulay enquired how much he owed.
"Oh, sir," said the barber, "whatever you usually
give the person who shaves you." "In that case,"
said Macaulay, "I should give you a great gash on
each cheek." This unhandiness made him helpless
in all games, and unable to swim, drive, or ride.
Once, when, as a cabinet minister, he was in attend-
ance at Windsor Castle, he was told that a horse was
at his disposal. "If her Majesty wishes to see me
ride," he said, "she must order out an elephant."
The only exercise in which he could be said to beat
everyone else, was that of walking the crowded
streets of London, his eyes glued to a book and
reading a great deal faster than anyone else could
read sitting still.

Macaulay's essay on *Milton*, his first contribu-
tion to *The Edinburgh Review*, had now made him
famous and he had come to live in London in
chambers of his own. This wider popularity also
opened to him the door of the House of Commons,
which he entered as the member for Calne. He
continued, however, in the closest relationship with
his home. In nature he was singularly affectionate,
and sincere almost to a fault; for he refused to live
upon terms of outside intimacy with people he
could not really.honour and esteem. But to those
whom he really loved, like his sister Hannah (after-

wards Lady Trevelyan), he gave his whole heart. When he went home the fun became uproarious. Sometimes it was hide-and-seek, at others capping verses, in which art both he and his sisters excelled. When the moment came for him to depart he would stand on the doorstep, holding the front door half open, and then shout at the top of his voice a last rhyme, bang the door and go away laughingly victorious. He and Hannah had the most amazing acquaintance with the novels of the period, and when they talked of their own affairs they did so in the words of Jane Austen's Mr Collins, or perhaps Mrs Bennet. In after years when Hannah and he were in India, and she had married Trevelyan, her husband, who rarely read novels, used to wonder who were the queer people with whom his wife and brother-in-law appeared to have lived.

Macaulay talked well and almost incessantly. If at times his talk was too plentiful it was at least always entertaining. Sydney Smith, who also liked to hear his own voice, once said to Macaulay at a dinner-party: "Macaulay, when I am dead, you'll be sorry you never heard me talk," and on another occasion he alluded to him as "talk-mill Macaulay." But at one party the unexpected happened and Macaulay was silent. What had happened? The secret leaked out—it was the extreme stickiness of the pudding; and he could not move his jaws whilst eating it. The dish was known ever afterwards as "Macaulay's pudding." This constant flow of talk was sometimes vexing to others, for there was no book discussed which he had not read, and apparently no subject which he did not seem to know better than anyone else.

His pleasant life in London society was much to his taste, but he was still poor, and so when he was invited to become a member of the Supreme Council of India he accepted the offer at once. He sailed in 1834; and stayed in India for four years. His sister Hannah accompanied him, and when he came back, he had enough money saved to enable him to live in independence.

Soon after his return from India Macaulay was again welcomed to the House of Commons. He became Secretary of State for War and remained in the House until his defeat when he sought re-election as member for Edinburgh in 1847. Though the loss of this seat gave his friends and himself great pain, it has left us a legacy of the beautiful verses which he wrote in his chamber, whilst listening to the shouts of joy of his opponents. In the earlier stanzas of this poem, he tells us how one by one the queens of gain, fashion, pleasure, power, have swept past by him until the queen of literature claims his allegiance. To her he addresses these verses, calling her the mightiest and the best:

> Oh, glorious lady, with the eyes of light,
>   And laurels clustering round thy lofty brow,
> Who by the cradle's side didst watch that night,
>   Warbling a sweet strange music, who wast thou?
>
> "Yes darling; let them go," so ran the strain;
>   "Yes; let them go, gain, fashion, pleasure, power,
> And all the busy elves to whose domain
>   Belongs the nether sphere, the fleeting hour.

Without one envious sigh, one anxious scheme,
  The nether sphere, the fleeting hour resign.
Mine is the world of thought, the world of dream,
  Mine all the past, and all the future mine."

.   .   .   .

The last stanza of the poem gives the promise of reward from the queen of literature to one who choses the world of thought rather than that of fame.

Yes, thou wilt love me with exceeding love;
  And I will tenfold all that love repay;
Still smiling, though the tender may reprove;
  Still faithful, though the trusted may betray.

After his political defeat Macaulay retired into the more private life of a writer, and, although he afterwards re-entered Parliament, the greater part of his time and energy was given to communing with the "lady with the eyes of light." His *Lays of Ancient Rome* were already well known and still ring in the minds of every school boy and girl. None of us can forget the story of "How Horatius kept the bridge in the brave days of old." And in such throbbing verses as those which describe the march of the enemy upon Rome we seem to hear the measured tramp and to see the shimmering spears of the advancing troops:

And nearer fast and nearer
  Doth the red whirlwind come
And louder still and still more loud,
From underneath that rolling cloud,
Is heard the trumpet's war-note proud,
  The trampling, and the hum.

> And plainly and more plainly
>   Now through the gloom appears,
> Far to left and far to right,
> In broken gleams of dark-blue light,
> The long array of helmets bright,
>   The long array of spears.

But Macaulay's greatest book was his *History of England*. "I am nothing if not historical," he once said of himself; and when a chance of leisure came he determined to devote it to writing a history of England from the Revolution of 1688 to the death of George IV in 1830. He began the work with an introductory sketch of English history up to 1685 and the three long chapters in which this introduction is contained show his skill in presenting a vivid and picturesque view of English life in earlier centuries. Unfortunately, however, he died before he had completed his account of William III, and it was left for his sister, Lady Trevelyan, to make the last pages clear for the printers.

Macaulay had a very noble conception of his duty as a historian and writer. In his composition he worked as hard as Darwin did for clearness of meaning, and he sought to make each sentence not only perfect, but beautiful in sound. He had a liking for short sentences, and in the essays he makes use of them with much skill. In writing his history, Macaulay tried above all things to make dry bones live, and he therefore visited, not only the sites of famous battles, but also the lonely places where the common people had rejoiced or suffered.

THE PASS OF GLENCOE

One of his finest passages describes the little graveyard in the Tower of London where the traitors of England lie buried. Another famous piece is his account of the massacre of the clan Macdonald at Glencoe. We know the story of the cruel slaughter of this little group of Highlanders by their hereditary foes the Campbells. In some treacherous way William III was induced to give his name to a paper permitting this terrible deed, and, led by a Captain, the murdering men of Argyle took vengeance on their innocent neigh-bours. In his history Macaulay tells us how the lonely valley between the dark mountains looked the day after the slaughter.

Mile after mile the traveller looks in vain for the smoke of one hut, or for one human form wrapped in a plaid, and listens in vain for the bark of a shepherd's dog, or the bleat of a lamb. Mile after mile the only sound that indicates life is the faint cry of a bird of prey from some storm-beaten pinnacle of rock. The progress of civilization which has turned so many wastes into fields yellow with harvests, or gay with apple blossoms, has only made Glencoe more desolate.

Brief extracts of this kind give a slight idea of the grace of Macaulay's sentences, and of the vivid pictures he could draw of things long forgotten. It is true that he was apt to be led astray by his love of the picturesque, and to increase the height of the mountains which surrounded Glencoe in order to deepen the gloomy feeling of the desolate valley. But he took the greatest pains in collecting his material, and before describing the battle of Killiecrankie, walked twice up and down the road in order to find out exactly how long the English army took in mounting the pass which they were to descend much more quickly. "He reads twenty books," said Thackeray, "to write a sentence; he travels a hundred miles to make a line of description."

It is also true that Macaulay is always on the side of the Whigs and sometimes his bias leads him into error. It is therefore interesting that perhaps the best of his poems is *A Jacobite's Epitaph*. Here we may quote the last six lines:

> O thou, whom chance leads to this nameless stone,
> From that proud country which was once mine own,
> By those white cliffs I never more must see,
> By that dear language which I spake like thee,
> Forget all feuds, and shed one English tear
> O'er English dust. A broken heart lies here.

Macaulay was now the best-known writer in England; the Queen invited him to Windsor Castle, and any great house where he was likely to be met was pestered by people asking to be presented to him. In 1852 the Edinburgh electors made compensation to him for his previous defeat, by putting him at the head of the poll, so he had the pleasure of feeling that victory had come for him and his "glorious lady with the eyes of light," his queen of literature. It is good that this triumph came when it did, for seven years later, at the age of fifty-nine, he died. He lies buried amongst those whose books he loved to read, in the Poets' Corner of Westminster Abbey, near to Goldsmith and Johnson.

JOHN RUSKIN

LIKE Thackeray and Dickens, John Ruskin (1819–1900) was a child of London, and his earliest years were passed in a small red-brick house in Brunswick Square, Bloomsbury, now marked by a memorial tablet. An only child, he led a lonely life, for, besides growing up in the solitude of an empty nursery, he never went to school. His education was mainly in the hands of his mother, helped by his father and occasional tutors. She had very strict notions about the upbringing of little boys and, amongst other things, she would never allow John any toys. The only time he had one was when an aunt brought him a present of a scarlet Punch and Judy from Soho Bazaar. But these joys were quickly taken away and even sweets were forbidden, for in all his childhood he could only once remember having three raisins counted out to him. Later he was allowed to come in to dessert and crack nuts—for other people.

It was good for him that when he was four years old his family moved into the country, to 28, Herne Hill, where there was a garden, and where amongst the shrubs and trees John made for himself a playground and found in the flowers and trees imaginary playfellows. It was almost a country garden, for in it were avenues of fruit trees which he was taught to value for their blossom, not for their fruit.

Once at a lecture Ruskin told a story of how when he was a baby in his nurse's arms he wanted to touch the tea-urn which was boiling merrily. "My mother," he says, "bade me keep my fingers back; I insisted on putting them forward. My nurse would have taken me away from the urn, but my mother said, 'Let him touch it, Nurse.' So I touched it—and that was my first lesson in the meaning of the word liberty." The significance of this word was later to be the subject of many of his lectures and books.

Sunday at Herne Hill was kept very sternly. All the story-books were taken away, and this severe discipline influenced Ruskin all his life. For forty years, he tells us, he never ventured to draw upon a Sunday; and when he did begin, he found that somehow his drawing never prospered afterwards. Ruskin says this severe upbringing taught him how to be happy with nature. "To watch the corn grow, and the blossoms set"; he wrote in *Modern Painters*, "to draw hard breath over ploughshare or spade; to read, to think, to love, to hope, to pray —these are the things that make men happy." For, in Ruskin's view, God had placed the real happiness of the world in "the keeping of the little mosses of the wayside, and of the clouds of the firmament."

There is no doubt that this appreciation of the beauty of nature was first developed in Ruskin in his solitary days in the old garden at Herne Hill; it is the text of many of his written works; and it remained uppermost in his heart until the day when he was laid to rest by his beloved Cumberland lakes.

The regular teaching of Ruskin began at the age

of three, when his mother taught him to read, and to repeat to her, the whole of the 119th Psalm. She had a profound reverence for the Bible and looked upon every word of it as written by the hand of God. She would, therefore, permit no syllable to be changed, no word to be left out. Ruskin loved the Bible for its beautiful language and tells us that patient Job was his favourite character and that he detested fawning Jacob. He says that he owed the priceless knowledge of this noble poetry and literature to his mother, while it was his father who taught him how to love and appreciate the beauties of romance and art.

By trade Mr Ruskin was a wine merchant, and although engaged all day in his business, he found time to read aloud in the evenings. Scott, Shakespeare, and Byron were some of his favourites. He would never let his son look at a bad picture, or handle a poor book. "All this care," says Ruskin, "made me lead a very small, conceited, contented, Cock-Robinson-Crusoe sort of life, the central point of which it appeared to me I occupied in the universe."

Upon one event of his boyhood, however, Ruskin looked back as a turning-point. This was a present he received on his thirteenth birthday from his father's partner—a copy of Samuel Rogers's *Italy* illustrated with small engravings of drawings by Turner. Ruskin's enthusiasm for these drawings was the beginning of his lifelong admiration and praise of Turner's work.

Ruskin would perhaps have been a happier man

if he had had the wholesome training of a public
school, or even the fresh breezes and frank criticisms
of the inside life of an Oxford college. It is true
that he went to Oxford, but he was accompanied
by his mother, who lived in rooms opposite her
son's college (Christ Church), and every day he had
tea with her. In later years Ruskin used to tell
some amusing stories of his experiences of more
rowdy undergraduates. At his first college supper,
for instance, Ruskin, to the astonishment of the
older men, kept quite sober, and was able to make
himself useful in helping to carry four other fresh-
men head foremost downstairs. He had, as a matter
of fact, poured the ladlefuls of punch into his waistcoat instead of down his throat!

To the great joy of his father, he won the Newdigate prize for poetry, and it happened that when
he declaimed his verse at the ceremony of Com-
memoration the poet Wordsworth was present to
receive an honorary degree and "took kindly notice
of the young prize poet." Unlike most university
men, Ruskin did not there begin the chief friend-
ships of his life, and even the great Oxford Movement, which was then awakening much religious
enthusiasm and controversy, passed him by. He
makes no mention of Cardinal Newman, the lead-
ing spirit of the dispute, and, like Ruskin, one of
the great masters of English prose. His tutors,
however, discerned his unusual gifts and prophesied
that he would win for himself a high place in the
honours examinations.

Amongst the people of his own age he became

known as a youth with very considerable knowledge about pictures and clothes. About this time
he prided himself upon his fine taste in dress; and
for the coronation of Queen Victoria, he ordered
"a white satin waistcoat with gold sprigs, and a high
dress-coat with bright buttons." We are not told
the colour of the neckcloth, but it would almost
certainly be of the favourite bright blue he nearly
always wore in after life.

On his twenty-first birthday his father gave him
Turner's drawing of Winchelsea, and thus began
the collection of that artist's pictures which Ruskin
afterwards possessed. At the same time he was given
a handsome allowance, and the first use he made
of his newly acquired wealth was to buy another
Turner, *Harlech Castle*, greatly disturbing his
thrifty father by this extravagance. It was through
the dealer from whom this picture was bought that
Ruskin first met his "earthly master," and the
praise of Turner's works, of which a collection may
now be seen in the National Gallery, fills many
pages of Ruskin's books.

But in this his twenty-first year Ruskin broke
down in health. This was the result partly of too
much hard work and partly of his first unsuccessful
love affair. He had lost his heart to the daughter
of Mr Domecq, the Spanish partner in his father's
business. His wooing was not fortunate; and perhaps it is not to be wondered at, for he says he
tried to entertain her not only with love-poems,
but with his opinions upon the doctrine of tran-
substantiation, a solemn subject for lovers' talk.

She mocked him gleefully. When Ruskin heard the news of her marriage to another man, he went "staggering along down the dark passage," overcome with emotion.

To restore his health the family started for a tour through France and Italy. A special carriage was built for the party and it held pockets for every imaginable necessity. They changed their horses after every day's journey, and it took them six weeks to drive from Calais to Nice. After this illness Ruskin worked for his Oxford degree and soon afterwards began to write the book which first made him famous—*Modern Painters*.

The keynote of all his writing was beauty; he wanted to teach the world to find the beautiful in nature and in art. He felt it could be found everywhere if only men could be taught to see: "in the wondrous loveliness of a tree's buds against the blue sky, in the mosses of the wayside, in the marbles of Rome, and also in the broken fragments of a rock." He urged artists "to go to Nature in all singleness of heart—rejecting nothing, selecting nothing, and scorning nothing."

Both at home and when travelling abroad Ruskin aimed at making his life very regular. He rose with the sun and read a few verses of the Bible, making notes of the meaning of every word and discussing in his mind the ideas they suggested. This he advises us to do in all our reading for we "thereby enrich our vocabulary." He looked upon his writing as a piece of tapestry: "I knew exactly what I had got to say, put the words firmly in their places like so many stitches, hemmed the edges of the chapters round with what seemed to me graceful flourishes." In early days he often read to his parents what he had written on the previous day, just "as a girl shows her sampler." Also, like the industrious needlewoman, he unpicked and remade his sentences over and over again until they sounded to him perfect. "I remember," he says, "that the last half-page of the 'Lamp of Beauty' [in *The Seven Lamps of Architecture*] cost me a whole forenoon—from ten to two, and that then I went out to walk quite tired, and yet not satisfied with the last sentence." In *The Stones of Venice* there is a passage which he wrote out and corrected many times, and it is worth quoting to show his ideas of history, as well as of language:

Since first the dominion of men was asserted over the ocean, three thrones, of mark beyond all others, have been set upon its sands: the thrones of Tyre, Venice, and England. Of the First of these great powers only the memory remains; of the Second, the ruin; the Third, which inherits their greatness, if it forget their example, may be led through prouder eminence to less pitied destruction.

To working men and women he had also sermons to give. "Less work and more wages, of course: but how much lessening of work do you suppose is possible? Do you think the time will ever come for everybody to have *no* work and *all* wages?...Do you want her [England] to be nothing but large workshop and forge, so that the name of 'Englishman' shall be synonymous with 'ironmonger' all over the world? or would you like to keep some of your lords and landed gentry still, and a few green fields and trees?" Ruskin was a great reformer and his heart was set upon making a perfect England, and there is something very beautiful and touching in the great movement which he founded to bring about the ideal country.

His idea was that everyone should belong to the St George's Guild. This was to be a noble brotherhood of all men and women who were holy, humble and virtuous. The boys were to be taught to be good carpenters and the girls to be good cooks. Every cottage was to have a few good books and pictures. There were to be no machines worked by steam, no smoky chimneys, no high rents, no railways, no idle rich, no overworked poor in this enchanted land. To forward his plans Ruskin gave £7000 to purchase land, and work was begun on a few model estates. But Ruskin and his devoted followers forgot the outside forces which rule our world. All men, unfortunately, are not noble and industrious, and life cannot be delivered by rules and regulations from all the troubles which come from evil and idleness. Nevertheless, the effort has not been in vain, and Ruskin's "divine rage against iniquity" has given to us better plans for our houses and education, and higher ideals of happiness and health.

Meanwhile the author of all these schemes for the betterment of the world was facing a tragedy of his own which was to darken all the rest of his life. This trouble was the death of his beautiful Rose La Touche. Ruskin was nearly forty and

Rose only nine when they first met, and during long years of waiting she held his love. She did not, however, know of it until she grew up and did not return it until very near the end of her short life. His love-letters to her, perhaps the most beautiful things he ever wrote, were destroyed after his death. There is no doubt that the long strain of this romance did much to bring about the collapse of Ruskin's mind, which for many years interrupted his time of work.

He had settled at Brantwood, in the Lake country, before these mental attacks became frequent. His home stood above Lake Coniston and he had furnished it in the most artistic fashion. Every thing was chosen from the best models. When he was choosing a wall-paper for his study, he remembered a pattern he had noticed on a bishop's cloak in a picture in the National Gallery. He asked a friend to copy it, and his wall-paper was made from the copy. The picture hangs in the National Gallery where Ruskin noted it, and the wall-paper can still be seen at Brantwood.

In spite of disappointments and ill-health Ruskin remained young at heart, and there was a fascinating boyishness about his pleasures. He would descend to the kitchen at Brantwood to make geological experiments in shapes of jelly, using blancmange for the snow and ice, and amongst these stiff masses of food he would create a miniature Switzerland, the snow mountains falling into terrific crevasses, and illustrating the formation of the Alpine gorges.

All children loved him and some of his pleasantest
letters were written to little girls. Katie Macdonald,
aged ten, was a special friend. She had founded a
society for kindness to animals. Her mother had
read aloud to her Ruskin's angry words about the
cruelty of killing harmless creatures. So Katie
boldly asked him to be a patron of her society, and
he not only consented, but promised to give the
society an address. In the audience was a small boy
who enquired whether, supposing certain donkey-
boys insisted on kicking their donkeys, the rules of
the society would allow them to be given "a jolly
good thrashing." Ruskin rose amongst the small
boys and girls, and pronounced his decision that
if *all other* means had been tried in vain, the
knights of the society might be allowed to inflict
a "thoroughly good, sound thrashing."

One of the visitors at Brantwood tells us how on
a Saturday half a dozen little girls used to come up
to Brantwood for tea and a lesson. "He's a foony
man is Meester Rooskin," one of them observed,
"boot he likes 'oos to tek a good tea."

So all through life, Ruskin loved to bring happiness to others, and, still more, to show them the
way to get it for themselves. But his powers of
teaching were failing, and for the last eleven years
of his life the voice and pen which had striven to
reveal to us the beauties of art and nature were
silent, worn out in our service. His love of nature
was, however, with him to the end. He died at his
beloved Brantwood and lies buried near Lake
Coniston. A grave was offered for him in West-

DAWN AT CONISTON

minster Abbey, but in his will he had asked that
he might be laid to rest amongst the Cumberland
hills.

ALFRED TENNYSON

So many great men were born in 1809 that it may
be called the *Annus Mirabilis*, or wonderful year,
of the nineteenth century. Among the great men
were Tennyson the poet, Gladstone the statesman,
Darwin the man of science, Kinglake the historian
of the Crimean war, FitzGerald the translator of
the famous Eastern poet Omar Khayyam, and
Monckton Milnes, afterwards Lord Houghton, the
poet. On the other side of the Atlantic, too, it was
a famous year; for in it were born Abraham Lincoln,
afterwards President of the United States, Oliver
Wendell Holmes, the autocrat of the breakfast-table,
and Edgar Allan Poe, the story-teller and poet.

Alfred Tennyson was born on August 6 at
Somersby Rectory in Lincolnshire, a county which
he describes as

> grassy, wild and bare,
> Wide, wild, and open to the air.

His father, the Reverend George Clayton Tennyson,
was the eldest son of a large landowner, but had
been disinherited in favour of a younger son and
compensated by the gift of two family livings. His
mother was the daughter of the Rev. Stephen
Fytche, vicar of Louth, and to this town the boy

went for a short time to school. It was from his father, however, that he received most of his early education, and being free to roam about amongst the Rector's books he began to write poetry at an early age; he even attempted an epic poem of about five thousand lines in imitation of Homer.

In the poem called *The Palace of Art*, he afterwards wrote of his early home as "a haunt of ancient Peace"; in another poem he gives us a picture of the entrance:

> The seven elms, the poplars four
> That stand beside my father's door.

Elsewhere he recalls the neglected garden:

> With blackest moss the flower-plots
> Were thickly crusted, one and all:
> The rusted nails fell from the knots
> That held the pear to the gable-wall.

The large family who lived in the Rectory were all skilled in making verses, and in the winter evenings they sat round the fire weaving rhymes or telling stories. It is said that Alfred had a story about an "old horse" which it took him months to relate. Finally, the rest of the family protested, and it was brought to an abrupt end.

When he was five Alfred made what was perhaps his very first line of poetry. Lady Ritchie, the daughter of Thackeray, tells us how he was heard crying out as he was carried by a storm along the garden paths at Somersby: "I hear a voice that's speaking in the wind." This is the first record of nature whispering her secrets to him. He might

SOMERSBY RECTORY, LINCOLNSHIRE

have written of himself as he wrote of Edith in
Aylmer's Field:

> Her garden...
> Show'd her the fairy footings on the grass,
> The little dells of cowslips, fairy palms,
> The petty marestail forest, fairy pines,
> Or from the tiny pitted target blew
> What look'd a flight of fairy arrows aim'd
> All at one mark, all hitting.

It is this magic gift of hearing and seeing what
lies hidden from the eyes of other people that
makes men poets. But incidents of home-life, as
well as the wonders of nature, gave Alfred material
for rhyming. There is a story of a set of verses
which he wrote upon the death of his grandmother.
His grandfather paid him ten shillings for the elegy,
and added: "That is the first money you have ever
earned by your poetry, and, take my word for it,
it will be the last." The next earnings came through
a publisher at Louth, who offered Alfred ten pounds
for a collection of one hundred and two pieces
which were published under the title *Poems by
Two Brothers*. The authors were really three in
number, as both his elder brothers, Frederick and
Charles, joined with Alfred in this early venture.
They spent the money in making a tour through
Lincolnshire to examine the beautiful old churches
of the county.

Tennyson not only loved the woods, the trees
and all the beauties of his country, but he under-
stood the ways of the little creatures who made
their home amongst them, and in the last lines of

the poem *Aylmer's Field* there is a very intimate account of many of them that are well known to English girls and boys:

> And where the two contrived their daughter's good
> Lies the hawk's cast, the mole has made his run,
> The hedgehog underneath the plantain bores,
> The rabbit fondles his own harmless face,
> The slow-worm creeps, and the thin weasel there
> Follows the mouse, and all is open field.

These lines could only have been written by one who had lain quiet for hours in an open field watching the creatures play. When he was a boy Alfred could make the birds believe that he was one of themselves. One night he was leaning from his window and heard an owl cry. He answered "To-whit, Tu-who'o, Tu-ahit, To-wh'oo." In response to his call the owl flew into the window, entered the room, and remained there as his pet.

This gift for imitating sounds gives life to Tennyson's verses. In *The Charge of the Light Brigade* we seem to hear the roar of the guns as we repeat his lines:

> Cannon to right of them,
> Cannon to left of them,
> Cannon in front of them,
> Volley'd and thunder'd.

And in his dialect poem *The Northern Farmer, Old Style*, we can hear the old horse cantering along the highway:

> Proputty, Proputty, Proputty.

Very little news from the outside world reached the rectory of Somersby, but when Alfred heard that the poet Byron was dead, he felt as if the world had come to an end, and went outside, and in his grief carved the words "Byron is dead" on the sandstone rock.

When we think of the lonely life Tennyson led in his boyhood, we are not surprised to learn that he was shy. In 1828, when he joined his two brothers at Trinity College, Cambridge, he was so painfully afraid of strangers that sometimes on his arrival at the door of the College Hall at dinner-time, seeing the tables full and hearing the buzz of talk, he was too timid to enter and would turn home dinnerless. On one of these occasions when he was hanging by the door, Milnes, afterwards Lord Houghton, passed by, and Tennyson, looking at him, said to himself: "That is the best tempered fellow I ever saw." Soon he had this pleasant man for his friend.

Tennyson's college friends were a distinguished group, for of the famous men mentioned at the beginning of this chapter all except Gladstone went to Cambridge. They called themselves "the Apostles," and met together to talk and read papers upon all sorts of questions. Amongst them, but two years younger than Tennyson, was Arthur Hallam, the son of the famous historian, Henry Hallam. Alfred says that Arthur was "as near perfection as a mortal man can be," and the friendship which grew up between the two was to influence the whole of Tennyson's life and work.

Although Tennyson won the Chancellor's Medal with his poem *Timbuctoo*, he left the University without taking his degree. About this time his mind was much distracted by home troubles, and the death of his father led, some time later, to the breaking-up of the old home at Somersby. But the death of Arthur Hallam crushed his spirit most of all. Hallam caught fever whilst travelling in Austria with his parents. For some months afterwards Tennyson was too broken-hearted to work. But out of his anguish there sprang the desire to write a poem in remembrance of his dead friend, and Tennyson's song of grief for Hallam is given a place by that other famous song of sorrow, Milton's *Lycidas*. In the earlier stanzas of *In Memoriam* Tennyson explained how he came to begin his poem:

> I held it truth, with him who sings
>   To one clear harp in divers tones,
>   That men may rise on stepping-stones
> Of their dead selves to higher things.

And from the dead self of the mourning comrade, there sprang in 1850 *In Memoriam*, and its author, who already by the *Poems* of 1833 and the two volumes of poems published in 1842 had won for himself a place amongst writers, became at once the most famous of the living poets of England. The death of Wordsworth left the position of poet-laureate vacant, and Tennyson was chosen to succeed him.

The installation of the poet took place in November, and, in order to be suitably clothed for his introduction to Queen Victoria, he borrowed, as Wordsworth had done before him, the velvet court-suit of Samuel Rogers. Poets, indeed, are not often wealthy men, but the tide of fortune had now turned for Tennyson, and he felt himself rich enough to seek out his early love, Emily Sellwood, and marry her. They had been engaged ten years before, but both were poor, and Tennyson had felt that it was his duty to release her from her promise. Now, however, they were married at Shiplake Church and began their life at Twickenham. It was about this time that Carlyle, who greatly loved and admired Tennyson, wrote a description of him to an American: "A fine, large-featured, dim-eyed, bronze-coloured, shaggy-headed man is Alfred: dusty, smoky, free and easy, who swims outwardly and inwardly with great composure in an inarticulate element of tranquil chaos and tobacco smoke. Great now and then when he does emerge —a most restful, brotherly, solid-hearted man." Of Mrs Tennyson Carlyle wrote: "She lights up glittering blue eyes when you speak to her: has wit, has sense: and were she not so delicate in health I should augur well for Tennyson's adventure." There is an account of an evening which the two great men spent happily in each other's company, sitting on either side of the fireplace each puffing at a long white clay pipe and neither speaking a word. "Eh, Alfred, but we've had a good time," said Carlyle, as he bade his visitor goodnight after the two silent hours which they had enjoyed together.

Not long after Tennyson became poet-laureate, the Duke of Wellington, the victor of Waterloo, died, and the laureate was called upon to write a poem upon the great soldier. In it he not only gives us noble poetry, but records the true feelings of the sorrowing nation. The Duke he calls

> that tower of strength
> Which stood four-square to all the winds that blew.

And

> Foremost captain of his time,
> Rich in saving common-sense,
> And, as the greatest only are,
> In his simplicity sublime.

There is a stately rhythm in this poem which suggests to the reader the tramp of a multitude of feet at a hero's funeral.

Tennyson's longest poem, *The Idylls of the King*, contains a series of tales of King Arthur and his twelve knights of the Round Table, who, as they sat with their perfect sovereign around it, consecrated themselves to the labour of setting right all the wrong done in the world. Arthur asked his followers to take a vow to give themselves up to the life of unselfish chivalry which he had chosen for himself:

> The king will follow Christ, and we the king,
> In whom high God hath breathed a secret thing.

This secret thing was that spirit of holiness which urges men to aim at a perfect life. For a while the order of knighthood flourished. But after a time the high standard was lowered and sin entered into the holy band, and one knight after another became secretly false to his high vows. The very

pursuit of purity by men stained by the world
hastened its decay. This we take to be the meaning
of the story of the quest for the Grail—the holy
vessel which held the blood of Christ. The quest
was good for saintly knights like Galahad, but not
for men like the more worldly Lancelot. It took
them from the work which they could do, to
attempt what was for them impossible. They "were
following wandering fires." This is the reason why
Arthur saw in the quest of the Grail

> A sign to maim this order which I made.

It took worldly men out of the world and shut them
off from their fellows; and though they were in that
way taken out of temptation to do wrong, yet they
did not themselves grow in holiness. The proper
question to ask about a man's life is not how few
sins has he committed, but how much good has he
done:

> How dull it is to pause, to make an end,
> To rust unburnished, not to shine in use[1].

Meanwhile Tennyson and his wife had become
rich enough to live in a beautiful house in the Isle
of Wight, where in winter

> the hoary Channel
> Tumbles a billow on chalk and sand.

He had also a house near Haslemere and here his
wife died and he himself grew old, while his two
sons grew to manhood and went out into the world.
Here also he accepted the peerage which was
pressed upon him.

[1] Ulysses.

Up to the age of sixty Tennyson had written only narrative and lyric poetry, but when he was nearing seventy he astonished the country by becoming, like Shakespeare, a writer of dramas. He wrote the story in dramatic form of Queen Mary, then of Harold, who fought at the battle of Hastings, and later of the great archbishop Thomas à Becket, with the exciting story of his struggle against his king, Henry II. At the end of his life, however, Tennyson went back to the lyric, and in *Crossing the Bar* the aged poet bids farewell to his life on earth, as he sets out to sail across the great unknown sea of Eternity:

> Sunset and evening star,
>   And one clear call for me!
> And may there be no moaning of the bar,
>   When I put out to sea.

He crossed the bar on October 6th, 1892, and is buried in the poets' corner of Westminster Abbey.

ROBERT BROWNING

BROWNING was born three years later than Tennyson. His father was a clerk in the Bank of England and lived in a house in Camberwell. He had a library of six thousand volumes, so the boy grew up "as familiar with books as a stable boy is with horses." His mother, who came of a German family settled in Dundee, was deeply religious and laid much stress upon the keeping of Sunday, and spoke severely about the sins of theatre-goers and card-players. She also went to chapel regularly, and it is probable that when her son sat beside her in the family pew he was storing the pictures which we find in his poem *Christmas Eve*—"the fat weary woman," with her umbrella "a wreck of whalebones," and the "little old-faced, peaking, sister-turned-mother of the sickly babe," who trudged to chapel through the rain, adding "her tribute to the door-mat, sopping." There is also a picture of the "hawk-nosed, high-cheek-boned Professor" who mounted up

> By the creaking rail to the lecture-desk,
> Step by step, deliberate
> Because of his cranium's over-freight.

Robert was a handsome fearless child, and even at two years of age he showed signs of a liking for music, painting, and rhyme. The story is told that when his mother was pressing him to swallow some unpleasant medicine, she was startled by the boy shouting with the cup in his hand:

> Good people all who wish to see
> A boy take physic, look at me.

His first painting was a cottage which he drew with a lead pencil and coloured with red currant juice. His high spirits led him into pranks, and it was thought best to send him to a Dame's school to be kept in order. The mistress soon saw that he was no ordinary boy. She quickly taught him to read, and his mind was full of fairy stories which he made into plays for the other children to act.

Robert's quickness made the parents of the other children suspicious that he was receiving more than his fair share of attention, and the result of their complaints was that Mr Browning was requested to take his boy away.

The next school to which Robert was sent was kept by the Misses Ready, who had more advanced pupils to compete with him. Browning tells us that these ladies took a personal interest in the children's hair, which was daily oiled and brushed whilst they sang in chorus "Twinkle, twinkle little star," and other songs from Watts's hymn-book. He spent there, he says, "seven unhappy years," and, writing of these days in his poem *Pauline*, he likens himself to

<blockquote>
a god,
Wandering after beauty, or a giant,
Standing vast in the sunset—an old hunter,
Talking with gods—, or a high-crested chief,
Sailing with troops of friends to Tenedos.
</blockquote>

It seems as if these fanciful longings and dream-pictures were part of his musings when he was having his hair brushed at the Ready school, or as a small boy sitting on the floor of the home study:

<blockquote>
They came to me in my first dawn of life,
Which passed alone with wisest ancient books,
All halo-girt with fancies of my own.
</blockquote>

These wisest books of which he writes were probably the volumes which lined the shelves of the well-furnished library of his father's house. Here he spent many hours reading and dreaming, his fancies moving with the tale he was reading; for Browning could never separate himself from the people whose story he was writing. Whilst as a boy he lived and dreamed in this old library with its world of hunters, chiefs and gods, he used to set some time apart for the serious work of preparing himself to be a poet; and the best way, he thought, was to read through all the words with their meanings in Johnson's *Dictionary of the English Language*. This would have proved dull work to most boys, but Browning found entertainment in it.

He was twelve years old when Byron died. He did not, as Tennyson did, cut the poet's name on the rocks, but he was deeply grieved, and twenty years later he wrote: "I would at any time have gone to see a curl of his hair, or one of his gloves." In the first volume of poetry Browning published, *Incondita*, there is much which suggests that he had been reading Byron's verse. But there was also much in common between him and Tennyson, not in their poetry, but in their knowledge of, and delight in, flowers and animals. When living in Italy Browning could by a low whistle entice the lizards basking in the sunshine to crawl to his side. His pet geese would follow him about like dogs and nestle in his arms. His pockets were filled with frogs, toads, or any creatures to which he took a fancy. He loved to spend his holidays lying under the trees which stood above Camberwell church. Near him the shy birds would hop and alight on his body, as he watched their every movement with an eye which saw and remembered. In *Pippa Passes* he recalls those days:

> There was nought above me, and nought below
> My childhood had not learned to know!
>   For, what are the voices of birds
>   —Ay, and of beasts—but words—our words,
>   Only so much more sweet,
> The knowledge of that with my life begun!

In *Pauline* there are a few lines which show us still more vividly the magic power given to the poet of entering in imagination into the life of nature:

>   I can mount with the bird,
> Leaping airily his pyramid of leaves
> And twisted boughs of some tall mountain tree,
> Or rise cheerfully springing to the heavens,
> Or like a fish, breathe-in the morning air
> In the misty sun-warm water.

This gift of finding a way into the souls and minds of the beings of whom he wrote breathes life into all the poetry of Browning. He loved nature, but, as he often said, he loved men and women better. And this is one of the marks of his poetry to be noted in comparing it with that of Tennyson and Matthew Arnold.

Browning had none of the training of a public school nor the delights of companionship with men of his own age at the university. After his school-days at Camberwell came to an end, his parents engaged a tutor to help him at home, and for a few months he studied Greek at University College, London. His chief education, he says, he gained through travel, and his favourite journey always brought him to Italy. There, when he married, he took his invalid wife, Elizabeth Barrett, a writer of poetry like himself.

Mr and Mrs Browning made their home in Florence and there the only child, a son, was born. Here also Browning wrote much of his poetry—not, however, *Paracelsus*, published when he was only twenty-three, and regarded by some as his highest work.

The poetry of Browning is full of difficulties, and perhaps none of it is more hard to understand than *Sordello*, another early work. It is said that the famous writer, Douglas Jerrold, tried to read it when he was just recovering from an illness, and, failing to grasp its meaning, called out in alarm and horror, "Oh, God, I am an idiot!" He believed that his illness had made him mad. A puzzled reader once asked Browning himself to explain a difficult passage in the poem; the answer was: "Just take from it what meaning you like."

It must not be thought that the writer of this difficult verse was a dull, solemn man—far from it. Browning was, in fact, fond of fine clothes and was always well dressed, looking very much more like a successful bank director, or barrister, than a man of letters. He liked good food, too, and agreeable company; visitors who called at his home were welcomed with both hands.

For an example of poetry written in gay and rapid narrative we may turn to *How they brought the good News from Ghent to Aix*. In this spirited piece we find many characteristic qualities of the

verse of Browning, which distinguish it from the
work of other English poets. The poem is founded
upon his journey to Moscow with the Russian
consul, when they rode thither, going night and day
as fast as horses could carry them.

I

I sprang to the stirrup, and Joris, and he;
I galloped, Dirck galloped, we galloped all three;
"Good speed," cried the watch, as the gate-bolts undrew;
"Speed!" echoed the walls to us galloping through;
Behind shut the postern, the lights sank to rest,
And into the midnight we galloped abreast.

II

Not a word to each other; we kept the great pace
Neck by neck, stride by stride, never changing our place;
I turned in my saddle and made its girths tight,
Then shortened each stirrup, and set the pique right,
Rebuckled the cheek-strap, chained slacker the bit,
Nor galloped less steadily Roland a whit....

IV

At Aerschot, up leaped of a sudden the sun,
And against him the cattle stood black every one,
To stare thro' the mist at us galloping past,
And I saw my stout galloper Roland at last,
With resolute shoulders, each butting away
The haze, as some bluff river headland its spray:

V

And his low head and crest, just one sharp ear bent back
For my voice, and the other pricked out on his track;
And one eye's black intelligence—ever that glance
O'er its white edge at me, his own master, askance.
And the thick heavy spume—flakes which aye and anon
His fierce lips shook upwards in galloping on.

In this quotation we may see the minute care with which Browning studied the features of a landscape or the habits of a horse and his rider. It is interesting to notice how the story is told in part by facts, and in part by the omission of facts. He points to the three riders galloping along. They ride to a town; we know that it is a fortress for the gates must be unbolted; it must belong to friends for the watchman bids the travellers "good speed." Clearly the rider is a good horseman since he contrives to tighten the girths and shorten the stirrups without reducing the horse's pace, and the rapidity of this pace is suggested by the appearance of the cattle as black dots against the sun.

Boys and girls who love horses will notice how cleverly the poet has touched the picture of a horse at full gallop—the white froth falling in flakes from the lips. At the top of his strength he is rushing along, shoulders bent forward; one ear bent backward to hear his rider's voice: the other pricked to catch the sounds of the road: the head low, the right eye just turned back as if to find the wishes of the man.

This poem also gives a good example of what is called "anapaestic" metre. This means that we can divide each line of the poem into four divisions, known as "feet," and each foot has, as a rule, three syllables, and in each foot the accent falls on the last syllable: for instance:

Neck by néck, | stride by stríde, | never cháng|ing our pláce

The verse is lyrical, but many of Browning's

poems, including his longest, *The Ring and the Book*, are written in blank verse. *The Ring and the Book* is a very long poem, having about twenty thousand lines. When it was published a famous literary journal called it "the most profound spiritual treasure that England has had since Shakespeare."

A poem better known to boys and girls is *The Pied Piper of Hamelin*, which tells how the Pied Piper, who had

> a secret charm, to draw
> All creatures living beneath the sun,
> That creep or swim or fly or run
> After me so as you never saw!

charmed away, by his music, the host of rats that troubled the town of Hamelin:

> Great rats, small rats, lean rats, brawny rats,
> Brown rats, black rats, grey rats, tawny rats,
> Grave old plodders, gay young friskers,
> Fathers, mothers, uncles, cousins,
> Cocking tails and pricking whiskers,
> Families by tens and dozens,
> Brothers, sisters, husbands, wives—
> Followed the Piper for their lives.

The Mayor and Corporation, however, refused to pay the proper fee for this deliverance and the Piper took his revenge. He began another tune upon his pipe and this time all the children followed him out of the town till they came to the side of a mountain where

THE PIED PIPER OF HAMELIN

A wondrous portal opened wide
As if a cavern was suddenly hollowed;
And the Piper advanced and the children followed,
And when all were in to the very last,
The door in the mountain side shut fast.

Thus were the Hamelin folk severely punished for their ingratitude, and at the end of the poem Browning points the moral:

So, Willy, let me and you be wipers
Of scores out with all men—especially pipers:
And, whether they pipe us free, from rats or from mice,
If we've promised them aught, let us keep our promise.

In *Rabbi Ben Ezra* we meet a wise, just, tender old man. The Rabbi is an aged Jew grown good and wise through much pain and sorrow. Browning in this poem seeks to show to us his belief, that even out of evil good can come and that characters are ennobled by suffering:

Then, welcome each rebuff
That turns earth's smoothness rough,
Each sting that bids nor sit, nor stand, but go!
Be our joys three-parts pain.
Strive, and hold cheap the strain:
Learn, nor account the pang: dare, never grudge the throe.

In Pippa we have a pure soul shadowed by the dark workers of evil. *Pippa Passes* is a poem about a little mill-girl working in the factories of a rich merchant lady who has a fine home in Asolo. One day a year is given as a holiday to her workers and Pippa, eager to make the most of her happy freedom, thinks she will go out to beautiful Asolo and see

4—2

the home of her employer. It is mid-day and the shutters of the mansion are closed. Pippa wanders up and down in front of them, picturing to herself the peace and joy which lies behind the darkened windows:

> The year's at the spring
> And day's at the morn;
> Morning, at seven;
> The hill-side's dew-pearled;
> The lark's on the wing;
> The snail's on the thorn:
> God's in His heaven—
> All's right with the world!

The two wicked ones behind the curtains hear her childish voice, and Sebald says:

> God's in His heaven. Do you hear that? Who spoke?

And the temptation which he had felt to sin is taken away by the innocent Pippa's voice. He says:

> That little peasant's voice
> Has righted all again....
> ...God's in His heaven.

Ottima, who is a wicked woman, does not notice the change which Pippa's words have made in her companion, and coldly explains who the girl is:

> Oh—that little ragged girl,
> She must have rested on the step: we give them
> But this one holiday the whole year round.
> Did you ever see our silk-mills—their inside?

The moral of the tale is that shoeless, half-starved, overworked Pippa is both happier and nearer to heaven than her rich, idle mistress. The joy of evil subdued, the triumph of suffering bravely borne, and the triumph of love over hate, of truth over falseness, are the lessons Browning tried to learn in life, and in that farewell poem which was published at the moment of his own death, he calls out to us as he crosses the dark river the words of his faith:

> One who never turn'd his back but march'd breast
>   forward,
>   Never doubted clouds would break,
> Never dream'd, though right were worsted, wrong
>   would triumph,
> Held we fall to rise, are baffled to fight better,
>   Sleep to wake.

He died in Venice just as the wires were sending him a message telling him of the favourable reception of his last poem. His body was taken at first to be buried on the island of San Michele, a flotilla of gondolas following behind the funeral barge. Two days later it was brought home to England and laid in the poets' corner of Westminster Abbey.

ELIZABETH BARRETT BROWNING

ELIZABETH BARRETT was born in 1806, six years before Robert Browning. Her girlhood was spent at Hope End near Ledbury, where her father, a rich Indian merchant, had built himself a home with Moorish windows filled with stained glass. One of

these let the light into Elizabeth's bedroom, which
she has pictured for us in verse:

> The walls
> Were green, the carpet was pure green, the straight
> Small bed was curtained greenly, and the folds
> Hung green about the window which let in
> The outdoor world with all its greenery.
> You could not push your head out and escape
> A dash of dawn-dew from the honeysuckle.

From this room she would in the night creep out

> To slip downstairs through all the sleepy house
> As mute as any dream, then escape...
> And wander on the hills an hour or two,
> Then back again before the house should stir.

She and her friends played in the day-time
making gardens, and Elizabeth loved to grow
flowers on the beds in the shape of a man. She
would sow the seeds to make him coats of deep brown
pansies, and waistcoats of gay pinks, and always for
his eyes there must be deep blue gentians. She had
a wonderful gift for learning and, as a fairy-like
little figure of eight, used to sit on cushions propped
up against the wall of her room writing verses. A
tutor was engaged to teach her Greek and she sat
reading Homer with a book in one hand and a
doll in the other. At eleven she had finished her
epic poem *Marathon*, which her father proudly
printed. Her grandmother did not approve of all
this reading and writing, and used to say that she
would far rather see Elizabeth hemming her dusters
more carefully. However, in spite of her know-

ledge she was a very happy little girl, playing hide-and-seek, or flying along the lanes on "Moses," her little black pony, her long dark ringlets hanging down each side of her pale face. But one day an accident happened which ended all this joy; as she was trying to saddle her pony in a field, she fell and the saddle rolled on top of her, severely injuring her spine, and taking away from her all power to move. For months she lay on her back. Soon after this her mother died, and her father, having lost much of his money, had to sell the beloved Hope End, with its beautiful hills and trees, and move his family to a house in London.

Elizabeth, though now an invalid, continued to write poetry, and when she was twenty-six *Prometheus Bound* was published, and one year later *The Seraphim*. Then another great sorrow befell her. Very unwillingly she had been taken to Torquay for a change of air, and there, during her visit, her beloved brother, who had come down to see her, was accidentally drowned. This grief, she wrote, "gave a nightmare to her life for ever," and the moan of the sea beating the shore sounded in her ears like his funeral dirge.

From this time onward Miss Barrett led a very quiet life. She hated to see strangers, and her habits of living, she said, "were like those of a bird in a cage, and he would have as good a story as I had." But at the very moment when her future looked most dark, a fairy prince was coming to give her all the joys of the gayest singing bird, and to carry her away with him to the south.

One day, her cousin, Mr Kenyon, brought the poet Robert Browning to see her. They knew each other's writings, but had not met. In a short time they became lovers, but her father would not listen to an engagement. "I have no objection to the young man," he said, "but my daughter should have been thinking of another world." However, he managed to see her three times a week without Mr Barrett's knowledge. Matters, however, came to a head when the doctor ordered her to Italy for her health. Robert Browning took her affairs into his own hands, and early one morning Elizabeth was helped by her maid to climb the altar steps of St Pancras Church, and there Browning made her his wife. The marriage was kept secret, and a week later Mrs Browning crept away from her home while her family were at dinner; her husband was waiting for her and they left the country for Italy.

Although Mr Barrett came to know what a happy married life his daughter enjoyed and that her health had greatly improved, nothing would ever reconcile him to her marriage. They, therefore, never met again, for she felt she could not come back to a home where she was not welcome. Perhaps there has never been another marriage of two such poets. When Wordsworth died, there had been some who thought that Miss Barrett should be chosen to fill his place as poet-laureate.

Her husband's love not only crowned her life with happiness, but inspired her to write the noblest poetry. Her *Sonnets from the Portuguese* are like the exquisite melody which an imprisoned bird would pour out in joy at the recovery of his freedom. Many great men have given expression in the finest verse to their feelings of love, but Mrs Browning is the only woman who has used the highest gifts of poetry in making us understand the beauty, the delicacy, the tenderness of a wife's heart. For this reason her work will always take a place amongst great poetry.

About this time a government commission was appointed to enquire into the cruel treatment of little children by the great mill-owners of Lancashire. When Mrs Browning read its report, her heart was touched by the account it gave of the starving factory hands and the misery endured by the boys and girls who were forced to spend long hours working in pits and factories. She wrote *The Cry of the Children*, an appeal to the world for pity for these English slaves:

I

Do ye hear the children weeping, O my brothers,
    Ere the sorrow comes with years?
They are leaning their young heads against their mothers,
    And *that* cannot stop their tears.
The young lambs are bleating in the meadows,
    The young birds are chirping in the nest,
The young fawns are playing with the shadows,
    The young flowers are blowing toward the west—
But the young, young children, O my brothers,
    They are weeping bitterly!
They are weeping in the playtime of the others,
    In the country of the free....

VI

"For oh," say the children, "we are weary,
        And we cannot run or leap:
If we cared for any meadows, it were merely
        To drop down in them and sleep.
Our knees tremble sorely in the stooping,
        We fall upon our faces, trying to go:
And, underneath our heavy eyelids drooping,
        The reddest flower would look as pale as snow;
For, all day, we drag our burden tiring
        Through the coal-dark underground—
Or, all day, we drive the wheels of iron
        In the factories, round and round."

Although this moving appeal seemed to bear no
immediate fruit, its noble words probably hastened
the Act of Parliament which led to the formation
of the Society for the Prevention of Cruelty to
Children.

The Brownings lived from time to time in various
parts of Italy, but they finally settled in Casa Guidi
in Florence. There their baby boy was born in
1849. The home of the two poets became the house
of call for many famous people who visited Italy,
and amongst these visitors was the great American
writer, Nathaniel Hawthorne. He tells us that he
found Mrs Browning curled up peacefully on the
sofa of her room, her little boy by her side learning
to read. She was a small figure, with pale cheeks,
dark eyes and ringlets of dark brown hair hanging
on each side of her face. At that time she was busily
writing her long poem *Aurora Leigh*, which she
kept hidden under the cushion, and wrote when no

one was present. Another American caller has prettily described her as "a soul of fire enclosed in a shell of pearl."

She died in Florence in 1861 and the citizens of the Italian city mourned for her, and erected a tablet to her memory on the front of Casa Guidi.

WILLIAM MAKEPEACE THACKERAY

IN 1815, when the great war against Napoleon was brought to an end by the battle of Waterloo, William Makepeace Thackeray, who was later, in his novel *Vanity Fair*, to tell us much about the famous battle, was just four years old. He was born in India and, like all English children born in that hot climate, was brought to England at an early age. He tells us that he could not remember much about India except its crocodiles, and the tall thin man, his father, whom he was never to see again. But little Billy, as his mother called him, never forgot the big ship in which he sailed home, nor the black servant who took charge of him on the voyage.

It was a very long journey in those days, for there was no short cut home through the Suez canal, so every vessel had to sail round by the Cape of Good Hope; furthermore, all the ships were sailing-ships, for steam-engines had not yet been generally adapted to ships. The vessel which carried Billy Thackeray home called at the Island of St Helena, where Napoleon Bonaparte was imprisoned, and in one of his books Thackeray says: "When our ship touched this island my black servant took me a long walk over rocks and hills until we reached a garden, where we saw a man walking. 'There is Bonaparte,' said the negro, 'and he eats three sheep every day, and all the little children he can lay hands upon.'"

Soon after Thackeray had come home to live with his grandmother, his father died, and then his mother married Major Henry Carmichael Smyth, a simple, charming gentleman, whom his step-son came to love dearly; he has, moreover, made all the world admire him in the character of Colonel Newcome in *The Newcomes*.

Thackeray was now sent to school. He did not like it at all, and long afterwards wrote of it in bitter words. It was, he said, "governed by a horrible little tyrant, who made our young lives so miserable that I remember kneeling by my little bed of a night and saying, 'Pray God, I may dream of mother!'" Charterhouse was his next school, and he named it Slaughterhouse, because the boys were so brutal to each other. Here he had his nose broken, and when the wound was mended his pretty face had quite lost its beauty. Luckily, by this time his mother and Major Smyth had come to live in England, and the lonely schoolboy had at last a pleasant home and a loving welcome awaiting him every holiday.

A great many famous men had been educated at the Charterhouse school and Thackeray was proud of being a Carthusian; when he grew up he delighted to remind us in his book, *The English Humourists*, that Steele, Addison and many other celebrated men had, as boys, cut their names on the desks and played around the walls.

Thackeray does not seem to have been a brilliant boy nor to have impressed the headmaster upon his arrival, for, after examining him, he was overheard saying to a junior master in a voice of thunder, "This boy knows nothing and will just do for the lowest form." The haughty chief little thought that the boy was one day to become a great novelist and to depict the headmaster himself in one of his books—*Pendennis*. In this novel Thackeray calls himself Arthur and tells us a good deal both about his own schooldays and his after life.

In his last term at school he wrote to his mother, "I really think I am becoming terribly industrious, though I can't get the Head to think so....There are but three hundred and seventy boys in the school. I wish there were only three hundred and sixty-nine." Soon after this he left, and was entered at Trinity College, Cambridge. But even here he did not learn much. There is no doubt that he was lazy; he confesses it himself, but adds that "all his faults were of the fourpenny order, and that the worst was indolence and love of luxury." Whatever they were, they prevented him from getting much good out of the university, and in little more than a year he left it and went to study at Weimar in Germany. There he was very happy, and in his volume called

Christmas Books we have amusing caricatures of the people he met. In *The Kickleburys on the Rhine* he calls himself Mr Titmarsh, and tells of his arrival on the banks of the Rhine and of the receptions in the royal palace of Pumpernickel, which is Weimar in the days of its ducal rule. Mr Titmarsh goes to all the tea-parties and the gay assemblies of the place, and meets the snobbish Kickleburys of London, from whom the little satire takes its title.

When Thackeray was twenty-one he came into a fortune inherited from his father, which gave him an income of £500 a year. He had long considered that his talents were suited to journalism, so he purchased the newspaper known as *The National Standard*. But his investment was very unlucky, and in a short time he had spent all his money. As he was now faced with the problem of earning a living, he started work as an artist in Paris and in most of his books we find pictures drawn by himself.

Just at the critical time when he had spent all his money, he became engaged to an Irish girl, Isabella Shawe. In twenty years, he said, they hoped to get married. However, their waiting was short, for he was unexpectedly given the post of Paris correspondent of an English paper, and their marriage took place at once. Once more ill-luck came; the paper failed, the little home in Paris was broken up, and the young couple came home to London to seek employment.

One of the first pieces of work Thackeray obtained was that of reviewing Carlyle's *French Revo-*

lution for *The Times*. Carlyle was so much pleased with the criticism that he sought out the young reviewer and has left for us this description of Thackeray: "a half-monstrous Cornish giant, kind of painter, Cambridge man, and Paris newspaper correspondent, who is now writing for his life in London." That was exactly what Thackeray was doing—"writing for his life." His London home, though humble, was a very happy one, for he had with him his wife and two little girls.

But these joys were not to last long. His wife's health failed and she gradually grew worse, until at last the light of reason died out of her mind. Though she lived for forty years longer than her husband, she never again knew anyone or took any notice of what was happening around her. When her illness became incurable, the small house in Great Coram Street was shut up, and the two little girls went to live with their great-grand-mother, "who found them too young." Their father, though he was broken-hearted, kept a loving memory of his short time of happiness, and long afterwards wrote to a friend about to be married: "Although my own marriage was a wreck, I would do it again, for behold, love is the crown and com-pletion of all earthly good. The man who is afraid of the future never deserved one."

It was about this time that Thackeray was in-vited to join the staff of *Punch*. He was one of its earliest contributors and for ten years he kept the world merry with his jokes and cartoons. He was never unkind, but he ridiculed falseness and sham and hated all forms of pretence. It was in *Punch* that he first began to write his essays on snobs. A snob, he tells us, is a "man who meanly admires mean things." It is a word with so many sides to it that perhaps it can best be made clear by a quotation from the description of a snob, which Thackeray wrote in days when a man was valued more for aristocratic birth or wealth than for goodness and virtue:

If you go down for five shillings look at the "College Youths", you may see one sneaking down the court without a tassel to his cap; another with a gold or silver fringe to his velvet trencher; a third lad with a master's gown and hat, walking at ease over the sacred College grass-plats, which common men must not tread on.

He may do it, because he is a nobleman. Because he is a lord the university gives him a degree at the end of two years, which another is seven in acquiring. Because he is a lord, he has no call to go through an examination...The lads with gold and silver lace are sons of rich gentlemen, and called Fellow Commoners; they are privileged to feed better than the pensioners, and to have wine with their victuals, which the latter can only get in their rooms.

The unlucky boys who have no tassels to their caps are called sizers—*servitors* at Oxford—(a very pretty and gentle-manlike title). A distinction is made in their clothes because they are poor; for which reason they wear a badge of poverty, and are not allowed to take their meals with their fellow-students.

Though Thackeray wrote severely of the mean-nesses of people, he had a loving and tender heart, and in his daughter's[1] memoirs of her father, she

[1] Lady Ritchie.

tells how, when they were little, he used to write long letters in a big handwriting to her and her sister, using a different hand for each child so that they might know at once for whom the letter was meant. In one he teases Nanny about her spelling and says:

How glad I am that it is a black *Puss* not a black *Nuss* you have got. I thought you did not know how to spell nurse, and had spelt it en-you-double-ess; but I see the spelling gets better as the letters grow longer; they cannot be too long for me....I would sooner have you gentle and humble-minded than ever so clever. Who was born on Christmas Day? Somebody who was so great, that all the world worships Him: so good that all the world loves Him: and so gentle that He never spoke an unkind word. And there is a little sermon and a great deal of love and affection from Papa.

The Book of Snobs brought Thackeray fame, and he was able once more to make a home for his little girls. Ever afterwards he kept them with him, taking them over to Paris when his work took him there.

Very often the two little sisters sat as models for the drawings that were to illustrate his books, and it was to please them that he wrote the "fireside pantomime for great and small children" called *The Rose and the Ring*, and drew the pictures which fill its pages. This story is full of fun; in Chapter IV, for instance, we read how when the Fairy Black-stick came to call upon the Prince and Princess, Gruffanuff, the porter, "not only denied them, but made the most *odious vulgar sign* as he was going to

slam the door in the Fairy's face!" and how Black-
stick then waved her wand and Gruffanuff "felt
himself rising off the ground, and fluttering up
against the door, and then, as if a screw ran into
his stomach, he felt a dreadful pain there, and was
pinned to the door; and then his arms flew up over
his head; and his legs, after writhing about wildly,
twisted under his body; and he felt cold, cold,
growing over him, as if he was turning into metal;
and he said 'O-o-H'm!' and could say no more,
because he was dumb. He *was* turned into metal!
He was, from being *brazen*, *brass*! He was neither
more nor less than a knocker!"

Motley, the American historian, has left us a
description of Thackeray after he had met him in
London: "He has the appearance of a colossal infant,
smooth, white, shiny ringlety hair, flaxen, alas, with
advancing years, a roundish face, with a little dab of
a nose upon which it is a perpetual wonder how he
keeps his spectacles, a sweet but rather piping voice,
with something of the childish treble about it, and
a very tall, slightly stooping figure—such are the
characteristics of the great 'snob' of England."
It is interesting to read this description of
Thackeray by a man who knew him, but it is not
fair to call him either a snob, or a cynic, that is, one
who does not believe in the goodness of human
nature, and who sneers at and criticises everything.
When Thackeray published his novel *Vanity Fair*
some people thought that he was too hard upon
human nature, but he says that "he wrote of a set

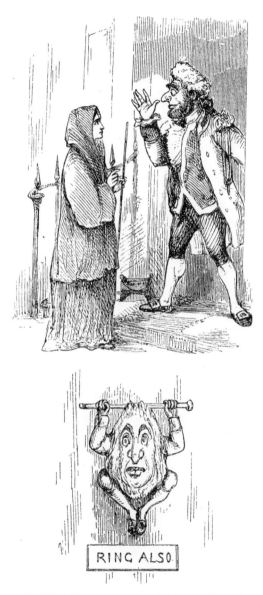

THE TRANSFORMATION OF GRUFFANUFF

of men and women living without God in the
world, greedy, pompous men, perfectly satisfied
for the most part, and at their ease about their
superior virtue."

In this novel we meet the disagreeable, but
clever, adventuress Becky Sharpe, the Sedleys,
foolish Amelia, and dear old Dobbin who loves
everybody. All these people are just what Thackeray meant them to be.

In his novels he likes to show us the wicked
people punished; thus in *Esmond*, the great historical novel which introduces us to the Jacobite
England of the Pretender, we read of the beautiful
young Beatrix breaking men's hearts in an easy,
careless fashion. At the end of her life we meet
her again. Her temper is soured, her face is
wrinkled; no one heeds her and she passes her
days in gambling and card-playing. Very different
is the picture of old age Thackeray gives us in *The
Newcomes*. It is an old age of poverty, for the
colonel has sunk from comfort to the poverty of a
pensioner of his old school, but he is not soured.

Thackeray wrote this novel while he was living
in Paris, and he was so deeply moved himself that
Annette, the cook, as he tells us, "came into the
salon to find me blubbering in a corner, I was
writing about the death of Colonel Newcome."
This is the passage:

At the usual evening hour, the chapel bell began to toll,
and Thomas Newcome's hands outside the bed feebly beat
a time. And just as the last bell struck, a peculiar sweet
smile shone over his face, and he lifted up his head a little

and quickly said, "Adsum!" and fell back. It was the word we used at school; when names were called, and lo, he, whose heart was as that of a little child, had answered to his name, and stood in the presence of The Master.

Before the end of his life Thackeray became well known as a lecturer; he was very successful both in England and America, and the money he made enabled him to leave his little girls a fortune. Thackeray worked irregularly, but when he died at the age of fifty-two he left behind him the fame of a great novelist and a lovable Englishman.

CHARLES DICKENS

ALTHOUGH DICKENS was six months younger than Thackeray, he made a name for himself in England much earlier, and Thackeray says with laughing jealousy: "I could not get near Dickens who is making ten thousand a year and he is very angry with me for saying so." The two novelists were rivals and though both were men of genius, those who read their books have never yet been able to agree which was the greater story-teller. Thackeray, who was a very sharp observer, noticed this at once, and wrote: "Dickens knows that my books are a protest against his—that is, if his are true, then mine must be false. But *Pickwick* is an exception, it is a capital book. It is like a glass of good English ale." When Thackeray died, Dickens wrote in *The Cornhill Magazine*: "No one can be surer than I, of the greatness and goodness of his heart."

Though Dickens was born at Portsmouth, where

his father was a clerk in the navy pay office, he was, like Thackeray, a true Londoner. Practically his whole life was spent within a circle drawn round London to include Rochester, Gadshill and Chatham. His father moved to Chatham when his son was four years old and there the boy lived until he was nine. As a child he was very delicate and unfit to play rough games, so most of his time was spent in his room reading over and over again the few books he had. He had a quaint little game of always pretending that he was the hero of the tale he was reading. All his life he was fond of playing this game of make-believe, and, had he wished, could probably have been a famous actor. Luckily for us, he was overtaken by a sudden illness upon the night when he was to be given a chance "to walk on" at a theatre.

At the age of seven Dickens was sent to a school which had fields and woods around it, where the boys could play. He was very happy there and spent many hours acting his tales under the trees. But suddenly things went wrong at home, money became short, and the family moved to a very poor house in a dull street in London. After this there was no more happy school time for Charles; instead, he had to help his mother to do the housework, to black the boots, and wash the dishes. There were now six children to feed, and the father, a kind man, but idle and careless, got deeper and deeper into debt, and finally was forced to go to prison—the famous Marshalsea, of which his son has written in *David Copperfield*.

When Mr Dickens was taken away to a debtor's prison, everything was sold, "even the boy's bed going for an old song," and Charles thought "what a dismal song it must have been to sing." In *David Copperfield* we have an account of the arrest of his father, who is depicted as Mr Micawber. He told David that "the God of day had now gone down upon him,...and his little son really thought that his heart was broken, but in the afternoon he was seen to play a lively game of skittles."

This was the most miserable time in the life of Dickens, and he never spoke of it if he could help. His mother and brother and sisters, having no home of their own, went to live in the prison with their father, whilst poor little Charles was sent to work in a factory for making blacking. His work was to tie on labels and to cover the pots neatly with paper, and his wage was 6*s*. a week. No wonder the boy was sad: he seemed to have lost all his beautiful dream-world for ever, and felt that he would never again have books to read, or happy hours of leisure in which to read them.

He felt himself to be a poor, neglected, forgotten child, half-fed, overworked, and poorly clad. In *David Copperfield* he tells us the story of the miseries he endured. Every Sunday he spent with his family in prison. Yet in spite of all he suffered, his observant mind was at work, and from this time onward he was storing in it pictures of the people who were later to appear in the novels and delight the world.

The Dickens family were luckily set free by a

legacy, which enabled the father to pay his debts and get work as a reporter. So, at twelve years old, Charles found himself once more a happy schoolboy, but with a knowledge of misery and wickedness behind him, which is rarely acquired by an old man. But this period of happiness did not last long, for in two years his parents took him from school and made him a clerk in a lawyer's office, very probably the firm which kept the accounts for Betsy Trotwood and employed some villain like Uriah Heep.

Having acquired a love of learning, Dickens determined to work hard and learn more, so he used to spend his evenings studying in the British Museum. He also, with much difficulty, taught himself to write shorthand. Then came the chance of his life: a reporter was needed for a daily paper and he obtained the post. He was now nineteen and found himself sitting in the gallery of the House of Commons working for his paper. In Johnson's days —nearly 100 years before—people used to report the speeches made there without having heard them, but by the time Dickens began his work, people insisted upon having an accurate account of what was said. This gave Dickens his opportunity; he had keen powers of observation and a fluent style, and not only did he write good reports of the debates in the Commons, but he also travelled about the country collecting news of what was happening in places far from London.

This side of his work was full of adventure and danger. In his day there was no telegraphic system by which news of country events could be rapidly

sent to the London newspaper offices. There were
very few railways, so the reporters had to travel
either on horseback, or in post-chaises which
travelled at about fifteen miles an hour, a reckless
speed in those days. Moreover, there was always
the possibility of an attack from some highway
robber, or of a drunken postillion, or of a break-
down in the snow. Yet Dickens never failed to
carry through the orders of his office, often writing
his paragraphs on his knee by the jumpy light
of a tallow candle, his mind continually disturbed
by the rumbling of the coach on the rough
roads.

Whilst he was earning his living in this way,
Dickens found time to write some little sketches
and tales which he signed "Boz," originally a pet
name for his young brother who had been nick-
named Moses after the vicar's son in *The Vicar of
Wakefield*. Laughingly pronounced through the
nose it sounds "Boses" and from that it became
"Boz," the name under which Dickens first won
fame as a writer.

In his own way he tells us how he came to print
his first tale which was called *Mr Minns and his
Cousin*:

"I had written a little something in secret, and
one night I dropped it, also in secret, into a dark box
up a dark court in Fleet Street." The story was
read and accepted, and when, in December, 1833,
Dickens saw his "little something" in print, his
eyes were so dimmed with pride and joy that they
could not bear to be seen.

The acceptance of Dickens's first tale was of great importance to the world, for it gave him courage to go on, and soon afterwards *The Pickwick Papers* came out in monthly parts. Only about four hundred copies of the first numbers were sold, but by the time that the fifteenth number was published the whole of London was talking about it. Everyone bought it, and read it, and people called their cats and dogs after the characters—Sam Weller, Jingle, Job Trotter, or Mrs Bardell. The book, moreover, brought to Dickens what was for him a fortune, for in the end he was paid about £3000 for it by his publishers.

The Pickwick Papers is not an ordinary novel; it has no plot, and is just a collection of stories and scenes loosely joined together. Most of the people in the stories are caricatures, and sometimes Dickens becomes so deeply interested in one of a man's peculiarities that he does not trouble to tell us about any other side of his character.

The Pickwick Papers are full of laughable adventures. Here is one about Mr Winkle: Winkle is a member of the Pickwick Club of which Mr Pickwick is the chairman. He is vain, and feels that there is nothing he cannot do if he tries. An opportunity arises in an excursion into the country of the whole club, to test the boasted sporting powers of Mr Winkle. He tries to shoot and only manages to hit a friend; then he mounts a pair of skates and falls off. There is not room for all the party in the carriage and so it is suggested that Mr Winkle might ride.

"The very thing," said Mr Pickwick. "Winkle, will you go on horseback?"

Mr Winkle did entertain considerable misgivings in the very lowest recesses of his own heart, relative to his equestrian skill; but, as he would not have them even suspected on any account, he at once replied with great hardihood.

"Certainly. I should enjoy it, of all things."...The principal [hostler] ran to assist Mr Winkle in mounting.

"T'other side, sir, if you please."

"Blowed if the genl'm'n worn't a gettin' up on the wrong side," whispered a grinning post-boy to the inexpressibly gratified waiter.

Mr Winkle, thus instructed, climbed into his saddle, with about as much difficulty as he would have experienced in getting up the side of a first-rate man-of-war.

"All right?" inquired Mr Pickwick, with an inward presentiment that it was all wrong.

"All right," replied Mr Winkle faintly.

"Let 'em go," cried the hostler. "Hold him in, sir," and away went the chaise, and the saddle-horse, with Mr Pickwick on the box of the one, and Mr Winkle on the back of the other, to the delight and gratification of the whole inn-yard.

"What makes him go sideways?" said Mr Snodgrass....

"I can't imagine," replied Mr Winkle. His horse was drifting up the street in the most mysterious manner—side first, with his head towards one side of the way, and his tail towards the other.

Pickwick is full of such lively scenes. It is also a wonderful picture of the time when it was written, with its account of old English inns and coaching adventures, of London law-courts and country elections, of the miseries of prison life and the

MRS SQUEERS AND THE BOYS OF DOTHEBOYS HALL

gaieties of the card-room at Bath. These and a hundred other scenes are depicted in a spirit of galloping fun.

After *Pickwick* there followed many more stories. In them Dickens showed his power of making people weep as well as laugh. He loved children, and could always see the world through a child's eyes. In his day the children of England were too often cruelly treated and made to work long hours in factories, sometimes as much as ten hours each day. Or, if sent to school, they were not given enough food. Dickens saw these and many other wrongs, and determined by his stories to make people ashamed of them. In *Nicholas Nickleby* we have the picture of a whole school being given a spoonful of brimstone and treacle to take away the little boys' appetites for their meal. Through the influence of the novels of Dickens many of these evils were reformed, and the children must always count him as their friend.

Towards the end of his life Dickens bought the house known as Gadshill Place between Rochester and Gravesend. He had known the house since the days of his boyhood, and had formed an ambition to live in it if he should ever be rich enough. Here he gave himself entirely up to the work of an author and public lecturer. He made a tour in the United States of America, where he lectured and gave readings from his own books. These drew very large audiences and brought him thousands of pounds. It was after this visit to America that he wrote *Martin Chuzzlewit*, in which book he sent his hero to travel in America. Some people regard this as his greatest work. It certainly contains the immortal Sairey Gamp with her brandy bottle and umbrella, the worst of all possible sick nurses. Besides amusing us, Sairey has done good, for the vivid picture that Dickens drew of her probably roused people to train a set of district nurses to take proper care of sick mothers and babies.

Dickens's habits of work were very regular: and although he wrote so many books his way of writing was very slow. "I go round my idea," he says, "much as you see a bird go about the sugar in his cage before he touches it." But once Dickens got into his tale he became absorbed, talking quickly in a low voice to himself, completely lost in the character he was creating.

In character he was singularly large-hearted, and no man ever lived nearer to the commandment, "Love thy neighbour as thyself." His taste in books was good, but limited. His two favourites amongst the writings of his own day were Tennyson's *Idylls of the King* and Carlyle's *French Revolution*. Of earlier literature he knew the great novels best—*Don Quixote, Robinson Crusoe, Tom Jones, The Vicar of Wakefield*. He had one characteristic which the other novelists, Disraeli, Bulwer Lytton, Trollope and Ainsworth, all shared with him. He loved fine clothes. It is related that he appeared at a party at Holland House in an emerald-green coat with a velvet collar, cream-coloured waistcoat, mustard-coloured trousers, and black satin tie with a double diamond pin and a fine gold chain. He also had made for himself a waistcoat of black satin embroidered with many-coloured flowers.

The last novel he wrote was *Edwin Drood*. He sat writing it in his summer-house in the garden of his house at Gadshill. He had reached the exciting point in the tale when the hero, young Edwin, is murdered. Who committed the cruel deed will never be known, for the writer died in the middle of his work, his pen stopping its labours in the midst of a syllable. The last words of the great novelist can be read in that unfinished story. When Carlyle learnt that he was dead he wrote, "That good, highly-gifted, ever friendly, noble Dickens— every inch of him an honest man."

THE BRONTËS

A GRIM legend is related of the Brontë family in the seventeenth century: Hugh Brontë, an Irishman and the father of a large family, was once crossing in a ship from England, when the captain found an ugly little boy hidden in the hold of the vessel. He was about to toss it overboard, but Mrs Brontë, in the tenderness of her heart, begged her husband to let her adopt it. Though Welsh, as the child was named, soon showed his cruel and wicked temper, Mr Brontë became very fond of him; but in the end Welsh murdered and robbed his foster-father, and then seized the home and drove out his foster-brothers and sisters. Then, by false promises he induced one of the sisters, Mary, to become his wife.

As he had no children of his own to inherit the riches he had stolen, he adopted one of his wife's nephews, inducing the poor parents again by false promises to part with their child. They never saw their boy, whose name was also Hugh Brontë, again, and after fifteen years of slavery and starvation the lad himself escaped from his cruel master by jumping into a river naked. After many wild adventures Hugh Brontë ran away with a lovely bride named Eleanor McClory; and their son, Patrick Brontë, was born in a cottage at Emsdale, County Down, in 1777.

Whether the whole story of the wicked Welsh is false or not, it was this Patrick Brontë who afterwards became the father of the novelists. He grew up to be a weaver, but as there were no lights strong enough for him to work his loom in the evening, he spent the nights in reading. He worked very hard, never allowing himself more than four hours of sleep, and used to sit night after night in the chimney-corner reading Greek and Latin books by the light of the flames, or working out problems of Euclid with the blackened end of a split on the hearthstone. "Splits" were made from bog fir-trees and were held in the hand as a light while burning.

In time Patrick became a schoolmaster, and in 1802 made his way to St John's College, Cambridge, where he took his degree four years later, and was ordained a clergyman of the Church of England.

Six years later he married Maria Branwell, a Cornish girl, and after working for some time as curate in the parish of Dewsbury became vicar of Thornton, near Bradford. Here Charlotte, Emily and Anne were born. A few years afterwards Mr Brontë was again moved—this time to the bleak moors of Yorkshire; and there at the lonely vicarage of Haworth—made more lonely by the early death of their mother—his children spent their lives.

The Reverend Patrick Brontë was himself an author and a writer of verses, so the family were brought up to the business of making books, and story-telling was a family gift. In fact, a tale was told at every meal, and sometimes the food would grow cold while the children hung on to the lips of their father, as he told them the terrible adventures of his own father at the house of the wicked foundling Welsh. At supper-time the excited girls used to beg him to stop, lest they should be unable to sleep when they went to bed.

Like Christina Rossetti, the Brontë sisters began first to work with their pencils, and in their great love for drawing they nearly missed their true vocation of story-telling, but Charlotte always wrote tales and tells us that between her twelfth and her fifteenth year she had filled twenty volumes. Perhaps they were the tiny little black note-books which their father gave each child for scribbling in. In these they used to jot down the plays they invented for themselves to act. Charlotte had a great admiration for the Duke of Wellington, who appeared in all her dramas and never failed to come off conqueror. Occasionally a dispute arose amongst the children as to whether he, Hannibal, Bonaparte, or Caesar was the greatest, and sometimes they had to call in their father to settle the question.

In order to prevent the girls being shy he used, when questioning them, to make them wear a mask and, hidden under it, they had courage to speak out boldly. They must have been rather unusual children, for when he enquired of Anne, who was then four, what a child like her most wanted, she promptly replied, "Age and experience." Then he asked Emily what to do with her naughty brother Branwell. "Reason with him," answered the small girl of five, "and when he won't listen to reason, whip him." Finally he turned to Charlotte, who was seven, and asked her what was the best book, next to the Bible. She promptly said, "The Book of Nature."

The replies of these little people sound very priggish and we feel sure that we should not like them, but they were really very simple, only their life had been spent amongst books without games and with very little of the mirth which we call fun. Their chief outdoor joy was for the six of them to walk hand-in-hand towards the glorious wild moors round their Haworth home, inventing for each other stories of the rocks and streams. No human beings lived on the moors, but the children had taught themselves to believe in the giants and giantesses, the fairy kings and queens, and the

highway robbers with whom their childish fancy
peopled them.

The real troubles of their lives began when they
were sent to the Cowan Bridge School for the
daughters of the clergy. In Charlotte's novel, *Jane
Eyre*, we have an account of Maria Brontë there.
She is the Helen Burns who dies of consumption,
caused by too little food and warmth.

Miss Temple, the favourite mistress, invites
Charlotte, who is Jane in the novel, to tea. A tray
is brought in:

How pretty, to my eyes, did the china cups and bright
teapot look, placed on the little round table near the fire!
How fragrant was the steam of the beverage, and the
scent of toast! of which, however, I, to my dismay (for I
was beginning to be hungry), discerned only a very small
portion: Miss Temple discerned it too:—

"Barbara," said she, "can you not bring a little more
bread and butter? There is not enough for three."

Barbara went out; she returned soon:—"Madam, Mrs
Harden says she has sent up the usual quantity."
Mrs Harden, be it observed, was the housekeeper: a
woman after Mr Brocklehurst's own heart, made up of
equal parts of whalebone and iron.

"Oh, very well!" returned Miss Temple; "we must
make it do, Barbara, I suppose." And as the girl withdrew,
she added, smiling, "Fortunately, I have it in my power
to supply deficiencies for this once."

Having invited Helen and me to approach the table, and
placed before each of us a cup of tea with one delicious,
but thin morsel of toast, she got up, unlocked a drawer,
and taking from it a parcel wrapped in paper, disclosed
presently to our eyes a good-sized seed-cake.

"I meant to give each of you some of this to take with

you," said she; "but as there is so little toast, you must have it now," and she proceeded to cut slices with a generous hand.

We feasted that evening as on nectar and ambrosia.

The next chapter ends with the death of Helen in the arms of little Jane who has slipped into the sick-room, and into the dying girl's arms.

And I clasped my arms closer round Helen; she seemed dearer to me than ever; I felt as if I could not let her go; I lay with my face hidden on her neck. Presently she said in the sweetest tone,—

"How comfortable I am!—but don't leave me, Jane, I like to have you near me."

"I'll stay with you, *dear* Helen: no one shall take me away."

"Are you warm, darling?"

"Yes."

"Good-night, Jane."

"Good-night, Helen."

She kissed me, and I her: and we both soon slumbered. When I awoke it was day,...and Helen was—dead.

These are sad pictures of the boarding-school where the sisters were educated; but not many comforts could be expected when all that was charged for the board and lodging of each sister was £14 a year.

After the death of Maria, Charlotte took the place of the eldest daughter, and laboured very seriously at her work of story-writing. During the holidays she carried this on chiefly in the kitchen, whilst Tabby, the maid, prepared the food, Emily swept the rooms, and Anne washed the dishes.

In spite of all the play-acting and scribbling, the

girls were very fond of housework, and sewed and knitted with particular fineness; Charlotte, especially, loved neat boots and shoes and pretty dresses. Her second school was at Roe Head, and when she left it she started to work as a teacher in the school in Brussels of which she has given us an account in her novel *The Professor*. Later her sisters joined her there, and in time they hoped to set up a school of their own at Haworth. The drinking habits of their brilliant brother Branwell unfortunately forced the sisters to give up this idea, so Charlotte returned to her teaching in Brussels and Emily stayed at home to keep her father's house.

Emily had, perhaps, the most powerful brain of the three, but she has only left us *Wuthering Heights* and a few poems. All the sisters wrote verses, but only those of Emily were truly great. Charlotte, finding them in a note-book, sent them with her own to the poet Southey. He wrote kindly of them to her but added that "literature cannot be the business of a woman's life, and it ought not to be."

In spite of this snub, however, the three sisters printed a small book of their own poetry. Some of the pieces by Emily are very beautiful; and very beautiful also are some that were not printed till after she was dead. One of these, *The Visionary*, had for its subject the lighted lamp on her table:

Silent is the house: all are laid asleep:
One alone looks out o'er the snow-wreaths deep,
Watching every cloud, dreading every breeze
That whirls the wildering drift, and bends the
    groaning trees.

Cheerful is the hearth, soft the matted floor;
Not one shivering gust creeps through pane or door;
The little lamp burns straight, its rays shoot strong
        and far:
I trim it well, to be the wanderer's guiding-star.

These lines give us a wonderfully vivid picture of the winter cold without, and the cosy atmosphere within, but the greatest of the poems of Emily Brontë was written in her thirtieth year, just before she died:

No coward soul is mine,
No trembler in the world's storm-troubled sphere:
I see Heaven's glories shine,
And faith shines equal, arming me from fear.

There is not room for death,
Nor atom that his might could render void:
THOU—THOU art BEING and BREATH,
And what THOU ART may NEVER be destroy'd.

In her novel *Shirley* Charlotte has probably given us in the heroine a picture of what Emily might have been, had her life been easier and happier. Shirley herself, with her laughter-loving, fiery nature, would probably have become in the lonely home amongst the Yorkshire moors as dark and tragic as Emily, who loved their desolate grandeur and passionately refused to leave them. She must have been wonderfully courageous, for a story is told of a mad dog biting her, a savage brute. She told no one of what had happened and also applied the cautery to the wound herself. Another time she thrashed her own bulldog,

Keeper, with bare hands until she had conquered him, though she had been warned that he would certainly spring at the throat of anyone who struck him. After her death, Charlotte wrote of her: "She was stronger than a man, simpler than a child, her nature stood alone."

Branwell the brother was dead; his going was a relief to all; but when Emily went, and then the gentle Anne, Charlotte felt very lonely. But her own life did not last much longer.

She had many offers of marriage, but at last Mr Nicholls, her father's curate, whom she has made famous as Mr Macarthney in *Shirley*, where she is Lucy Snowe, was accepted. He had long loved her and valued her genius. He roared with laughter at the picture she had drawn of himself and other curates. There is no doubt that most of her creations are taken from real life. Helstone, in the same novel, is her father with his delight in soldiers. In *The Professor* Charlotte transports us to her life in Belgium and introduces us to the simpering, heated, emotional nature of the school-girls of Brussels with their acute worldly head mistress, and the absent-minded professor. Fortunately, her married life was happy—but all too brief. She was married to Mr Nicholls in June, 1854, and on March 31st of the next year she died.

GEORGE ELIOT

WARWICKSHIRE, which may proudly call itself Shakespeare's county, can also claim the famous novelist George Eliot. For in a country district, about thirty miles from Nuneaton, Mary Ann Evans, the writer who liked to be known to the world as George Eliot, was born in 1819. Her home was near Arbury, and her father, who started life as a village carpenter, rose to be the land-agent of the Newdigate family, the squires of the locality. There is no doubt that the description of the carpenter in *Adam Bede* is a picture of the writer's father: "tall, stalwart, a Saxon justifying his name of Adam, with jet black hair made the more noticeable by its contrast with the light paper cap, and the keen glance of the dark eye that shone from under the strongly marked, prominent eyebrows, indicated a mixture of Celtic blood."

The home of George Eliot's childhood was a beautiful old house standing in the park of the Newdigate mansion, and is described in the novel as the Hall Farm, where Mrs Poyser ruled. The reader is bidden to look inside:

Put your face to one of the glass panes in the right-hand corner and what do you see?...the dairy: it was certainly well worth looking at:—such coolness, such purity, such fragrance of new-pressed cheese, of firm butter, of wooden vessels perpetually bathed in pure water: such soft colourings of earthenware and creamy surfaces, brown wood, and polished grey lime-stone and rich orange-red rust on the iron weights and hooks and hinges.

From the outside, the Hall Farm house was a low-roofed dwelling with flat fields stretching southward, a cosy little place with neat, well-kept gardens. Every day the great coach running from Birmingham to London passed the gate, and as little children Mary Ann and her only brother watched it roll by with wondering excitement. In *The Mill on the Floss* we hear a great deal about these childish days. In it she calls herself Maggie and her brother Tom Tulliver. They wander about together fishing, spinning tops, playing marbles, gathering earth-nuts. They would, no doubt, have played cricket or football, but in those times no one knew much about such games. Maggie was a sore trouble to her mother because of her boyish ways. In the novel Mrs Tulliver complains bitterly of her:

"But her hair won't curl all I can do with it, and she's so franzy about having it put i' paper, and I've such work as niver was to make her stand and have it pinched with th' irons."

"Cut it off—cut it off short," said the father, rashly.

"How can you talk so, Mr Tulliver? She's too big a gell—gone nine, and tall of her age, to have her hair cut short; an' there's her cousin Lucy's got a row of curls round her head, an' not a hair out o' place. It seems hard as my sister Deane should have that pretty child; I'm sure Lucy takes more after me nor my own child does. Maggie, Maggie," continued the mother, in a tone of half-coaxing fretfulness, as this small mistake of nature entered the room. "Where's the use o' my telling you to keep away from the water? You'll tumble in and be drownded some day, an' then you'll be sorry you didn't do as mother told you."

Maggie's hair, as she threw off her bonnet, painfully confirmed her mother's accusation.

"Oh dear! Oh dear, Maggie, what are you thinkin' of, to throw your bonnet down there? Take it upstairs, there's a good gell, an' let your hair be brushed, an' put your other pinafore on, an' change your shoes—do, for shame: an come an' go on with your patchwork, like a little lady."

"Oh, mother," said Maggie, in a vehemently cross tone, "I don't *want* to do my patchwork."

"What! not your pretty patchwork, to make a counter-pane for your aunt Glegg?"

"It's foolish work," said Maggie, with a toss of her mane, "tearing things to pieces to sew 'em together again. And I don't want to do anything for my aunt Glegg—I don't like her."

Exit Maggie, dragging her bonnet by the string, while Mr Tulliver laughs audibly.

This happy, childish time ends in the departure of Tom to boarding-school, and Maggie is left in proud care of his rabbits. These she unfortunately forgets to feed, and there is trouble when he comes home for his holidays and finds them all dead.

Tom stopped immediately in his walk and turned round towards Maggie.

"You forgot to feed 'em....You're a naughty girl," said Tom, severely, "and I'm sorry I bought you the fish-line. I don't love you."

"Oh, Tom, it's very cruel," sobbed Maggie. "I'd forgive you, if *you* forgot anything—I wouldn't mind what you did—I'd forgive you and love you."

"Yes, you're a silly—but I never *do* forget things—*I* don't."

"Oh, please forgive me, Tom; my heart will break,"

said Maggie, shaking with sobs, clinging to Tom's arm, and laying her wet cheek on his shoulder.

Tom shook her off, and stopped again, saying in a peremptory tone, "Now, Maggie, you just listen. Aren't I a good brother to you?"

"Ye—ye—es," sobbed Maggie, her chin rising and falling convulsedly...."Ye—ye—es and I...lo—lo—love you so, Tom."

"But you're a naughty girl. Last holidays you licked the paint off my lozenge-box, and the holidays before that you let the boat drag my fish-line down when I'd set you to watch it and you pushed your head through my kite, all for nothing."

"But I didn't mean," said Maggie; "I couldn't help it."

"Yes, you could," said Tom, "if you'd minded what you were doing. And you're a naughty girl, and you shan't go fishing with me to-morrow."

With this terrible conclusion Tom ran away from Maggie towards the mill. Maggie stood motionless, except from her sobs, for a minute or two; then she turned round and ran into the house, and up to her attic, where she sat on the floor, and laid her head against the worm-eaten shelf with a crushing sense of misery.

When she was twelve, this little misunderstood girl went to school, but at sixteen her mother died and she had to come home and keep her father's house. Although, like Maggie Tulliver, George Eliot hated sewing as a child, she became a famous needlewoman, and her dairy in her father's house was as sweet and clean as the one she showed us when we peeped into the windows of Mrs Poyser's farm. And in butter-making she earned fame in Coventry market.

Not only did Miss Evans look after her father's

house, but she also found time to carry on her own studies in music, French, Italian, German, Greek and Latin. At this time she was a religious and very serious young woman, inclined to disapprove of theatre-going, novel-reading, and fine clothes. As she grew older she became less severe, and gradually found much delight in the pleasures she had formerly looked upon as wicked.

Her father died when she was thirty and then the life at the home farm ended. Mary Ann now determined to live abroad and study languages and, above all, make herself acquainted with the beautiful pictures and fine scenery of other lands. She began also to write, and from time to time her articles were printed in the English magazines. She gradually won her way in the world of letters, editors believing that it was a man who wrote the learned translations of theological and philosophical works. Some time after she returned to England she was invited to become assistant editor of *The Westminster Review*. She boarded in the same house as the editor, and in this way made the acquaintance of Herbert Spencer and Carlyle. Carlyle made friends with her, so that she might perhaps, through her magazine, help him to get recognition for the young unknown poet, Robert Browning. She was now living in the midst of literary society and had become a person of great power on the staff of the magazine.

In the beginning she had felt too shy to write under her own name, and so *Amos Barton*, the first tale in *Clerical Reminiscences*, was sent to the publisher Blackwood by a friend who said that it was the work of a modest young writer named George Eliot. The firm accepted the work and believed that the writer was a clergyman. It was not until two years later, when an impostor claimed to be George Eliot, that the real George Eliot revealed herself to her publisher.

The story of *Amos Barton* was brilliantly successful, and when all the tales were gathered together under the name *Scenes of Clerical Life*, the book became very popular.

The next book was *Adam Bede*, and for the copyright of this the author received eight hundred pounds. It was, as we know, the story of the country in which she spent her youth when her home was at the Hall Farm, and everyone who read the book was charmed by its simple, humorous characters. In a few weeks the world was talking of it, and the sayings of Mrs Poyser were quoted in the House of Commons.

The Mill on the Floss, the book which contains the story of Tom and Maggie Tulliver, came next; and a year later *Silas Marner*, another glimpse into simple village history, appeared. *Silas Marner* is the tale of a miserly old bachelor who finds a friendless baby on his doorstep and, to the amazement of his neighbours, adopts it.

After this there came a break in George Eliot's work. She went to Italy to try to make herself familiar with the famous Florentine monk, Savonarola, who preached in the Cathedral of Florence in the sixteenth century. She was so deeply moved by the old monk's sermons and by his angry wrath at the wickedness of his native city that she longed to weave a romance around him, and *Romola* gives us a picture both of the power Savonarola had over the nobles of Florence and also of the mean people by whom he was surrounded. At that period great respect was paid in Italy to learning, and the penniless hero of the story wins his way to the front place in the city because of his classical knowledge, but falls to pieces when his true character is revealed. The strain of writing the book was very heavy. George Eliot says that she felt a young woman when she started to write *Romola* and knew herself to be an old one when it was finished.

It marks the change in her work. It may be that, having used all the homely stories of her own life, she had not enough imagination to create new characters as attractive as the Tullivers, Poysers and Bedes. Whatever the cause may be, the fact remains that *Romola* did not make the same wide appeal as her other books had done.

In her next novel, *Felix Holt*, we are taken into the stormy atmosphere of an English political election shortly after the Reform Bill of 1832. Then George Eliot tried her hand at writing poetry; but no one cared for her verses, so she fortunately returned to story-telling and gave us *Middlemarch*, which is really two novels in one. It has two heroes and two heroines, who unfortunately marry the wrong parties. The old bookworm secures the lovely young Dorothea and fails to understand her or make her happy; whilst the man who was made to be her mate is married to silly, empty-headed Rosamond, who is as selfish as the scholar.

The last novel George Eliot wrote was *Daniel Deronda*. In it she gives us an account of the Jews. The book is of interest at the present day, for the hero is full of the idea of taking his nation back to dwell in Palestine.

Four years after the publication of this book George Eliot died.

ELIZABETH CLEGHORN GASKELL

CHEYNE WALK, Chelsea, has perhaps known as many writers of books as any street in England. Its greatest glory is, undoubtedly, the house where Carlyle and his wife lived. It is still to be visited, and we can sit on their chairs, read their books and letters, and even try on Carlyle's funny round hat. At one time they had for neighbours Leigh Hunt (whose wife was always borrowing tea), Rossetti, Kingsley, George Eliot, Swinburne, and Mrs Gaskell.

It was in 1810 that Elizabeth Cleghorn Stevenson (afterwards Mrs Gaskell) was born at No. 93, though the house was at that time known as 12, Old Lindsey Row.

Her father, William Stevenson, from whom she inherited her brains, was then on the staff of *The Edinburgh Review*, but he ended his life as Keeper of the Records of the Treasury. A month after the birth of his daughter, his wife died, and his motherless child was taken by stage-coach to Knutsford in Cheshire, to be brought up by an adorable maiden aunt, whom we all love as Miss Matty in *Cranford*. The tale of this great journey can be read in *Mary Barton*, when Babby travels from London to Manchester.

Elizabeth spent thirteen years in Knutsford. There she met, besides her aunt, the farmer, the sailor, the doctor and all the dear simple folk to whom she introduces us in *Cranford*. The story tells us how Miss Matty, after an interval of forty years, meets her first and only love, Mr Holbrook. They are in the draper's; she is buying silks and he is trying on woollen gloves. She accepts his invitation to spend a long June day at his farm house, and in a fly Miss Matty, her niece, and Miss Pole are driven there.

"What a pretty room!" said Miss Matty, *sotto voce*.

"What a pleasant place!" said I, aloud, almost simultaneously.

"Nay! if you like it," replied he, "but can you sit on these great black leather three-cornered chairs? I like it better than the best parlour; but I thought ladies would take that for the smarter place."

It was the smarter place, but, like most smart things, not at all pretty, or pleasant, or home-like: so, while we were at dinner, the servant-girl dusted and scrubbed the counting-house chairs, and we sat there all the rest of the day.

We had pudding before meat; and I thought Mr Holbrook was going to make some apology for his old-fashioned ways, for he began:

"I don't know whether you like new-fangled ways."

"Oh, not at all!" said Miss Matty.

"No more do I," said he. "My housekeeper *will* have these in her new fashions; or else I tell her that, when I was a young man, we used to keep strictly to my father's rule, 'No broth, no ball; no ball, no beef'; and always began dinner with broth. Then we had suet puddings, boiled in the broth with the beef; and then the meat itself. If we did not sup our broth, we had no ball, which we liked a deal better; and the beef came last of all, and only those had it, who had done justice to the broth and the ball. Now folks begin with sweet things, and turn their dinners topsy-turvy."

When the ducks and green peas came, we looked at each other in dismay; we had only two-pronged, black-handled forks. It is true the steel was as bright as silver; but what were we to do? Miss Matty picked up her peas, one by one, on the point of the prongs, much as Amine ate her grains of rice after her previous feast with the Ghoul. Miss Pole sighed after her delicate young peas as she left them on one side of her plate untasted, for they *would* drop between the prongs. I looked at my host; the peas were going wholesale into his capacious mouth, shovelled up by his large, round-ended knife. I saw, I imitated, I survived!...

After dinner, a clay pipe was brought in, and a spittoon; and, asking us to retire to another room, where he would soon join us, if we disliked tobacco-smoke, he presented his pipe to Miss Matty, and requested her to fill the bowl.

This was a compliment to a lady in his youth; but it was rather inappropriate to propose it as an honour to Miss Matty, who had been trained by her sister to hold smoking of every kind in utter abhorrence. But if it was a shock to her refinement, it was also a gratification to her feelings to be thus selected; so she daintily stuffed the strong tobacco into the pipe, and then we withdrew.

"It is very pleasant dining with a bachelor," said

Miss Matty, softly, as we settled ourselves in the counting-house. "I only hope it is not improper; so many pleasant things are!"

When Elizabeth was fourteen she left her aunt's tall red house to go to school at Stratford-on-Avon where she was thrilled by the thought of living in a house which had, in its earlier history, been one of the homes of Shakespeare. Meanwhile her father had married again, and when at seventeen she finished her education and returned to London, she found there a stepmother and a stepsister, Catherine. Her father, a gay, brilliant, easily bullied man, is almost certainly the original of Mr Gibson in *Wives and Daughters*, whilst Molly Gibson, who suffers much unhappiness at the hands of her stepmother and stepsister, is Elizabeth herself. Two years later William Stevenson died, and Elizabeth was free to return to her beloved Aunt Lumb and the delights of Knutsford.

She had now grown to be a most beautiful woman, as may be seen in the portrait of her by the famous painter Richmond.

Many men fell in love with her, and when she was twenty-two she was married to William Gaskell, the junior Unitarian minister of Cross Street Chapel, Manchester. In years he was only four ahead of his lovely bride, but he was twenty in experience. His duties as Unitarian minister took him into the midst of the poorest and perhaps most miserable working folk in the world; for Cross Street is in the heart of the slums of Manchester, and at that time the city was in the agony of an

MRS GASKELL

industrial revolution. Machinery had been invented which could turn the wheels of the cotton-spinning machines quicker and better than human hands; and the question was, What was to be done with the factory hands? To continue to employ the same number of men, women and children, was ruin to the owners; to send them adrift was certain starvation to themselves.

There is a terrible, unbreakable law in economics called supply and demand. From time to time, especially after the turmoil of a great war, men try to evade it, but in the end it must always be obeyed or else industry comes to a standstill, and there is no work, and no money to pay those who wish to work. Just when William Gaskell brought his young wife home to Cross Street, the poor folk who had been turned out of the mills were trying to beat down this cruel law. Why, they asked, should the labour which had been a livelihood for them and for their fathers and grandfathers, be given to machines?

Around the quiet scholarly home of the preacher the battle raged night and day: on the one hand there was the nightly burning of mills and breaking of machinery by the enraged workers, on the other the midnight drilling, by the mill-owners, of those who were on the side of the masters. In the beginning the sympathies of Mrs Gaskell were all with the factory hands, and from her bedroom windows she used, in the terrible days of the Chartist Riots, to fling bread to all those who were starving around her. Her home was in the storm-centre, and around her people were living under terrible conditions. Close by the chapel twenty human beings, on an average, were housed in two rooms,—"a ragged horde as filthy as the swine that live on the refuse in their streets." Such was the account given in the report made to the government by a poor law commission.

In the midst of all this turmoil and distress Mrs Gaskell lived and worked. Four children were born, and then she lost her only boy, Willie. This sorrow, coming upon the top of all the misery and starvation she was watching day by day, unsteadied her. She was ordered to leave Manchester, but Mr Gaskell could not move from his work, and she refused to be separated from him.

He had noticed how much writing seemed to soothe his wife's nerves and, in order to make her well again, he pressed upon her the idea that she could write a novel, and advised her to tell the story of what she saw going on around her. She was 37, and it was on the eve of the Revolution of 1848, that Mrs Gaskell gave her first story, *Mary Barton*, to the world.

It was a pathetic account of the poor crushed factory hands, and greatly irritated the rich mill-owners and learned economists, who could not understand why their theories of political economy had failed to set everything right. *Mary Barton* will always be looked upon as the book more than any other which started the world upon a new form of slave emancipation. The negroes had won their liberty, but it was Mrs Gaskell who, like Carlyle and Charles Kingsley, pointed out that the English people had, by their harsh legislation, created a slavery amongst their own people, as crushing and cruel as that which they had abolished in America, Africa and the West Indies. *Mary Barton*, with its simple story of sorrow and suffering, went straight to the hearts of English folk as a plea for the down-trodden Lancashire factory-workers.

In *North and South* Mrs Gaskell turned her sympathy to the side of the masters of the mills; and in her portrait of Thorton, the kindly owner whose factory was burnt by his angry workmen, we get another side of the sad picture of this industrial strife.

In all we have about forty stories from Mrs Gaskell's pen; but the best of them all is *Cranford* and, as we have seen, it is wholly different from her other work. It ripples with soft laughter from beginning to end, and when we think of it in literature we place it by the side of such masterpieces as the *Vicar of Wakefield* by Oliver Goldsmith or *Pride and Prejudice* by Jane Austin. Age does not lessen their charm, nor time alter our love for them—and that is the one and only test of true greatness in authorship. All three books deal with simple, unexciting events: life in a country parsonage, a walk in the lanes to a picnic, or a box of old love-letters written twenty years ago. Had Mrs Gaskell written more novels of the same quality as *Cranford*, she would take her place amongst the greatest English writers.

A fresh field of work was opened to her when

Patrick Brontë invited her to write the life of his
daughter Charlotte. The two women had first met
in 1850. A common friend invited both of them
to pay her a visit at Windermere. The contrast
between the two was noticeable. Mrs Gaskell
came into the room, bright, gay, quite at home,
talking easily, equal to anything. Charlotte Brontë,
who had arrived earlier, was a sad contrast, as she
sat nervously upon the sofa in her stiff black silk
frock, looking as if she wished the floor would open
and swallow her up. The two novelists, however,
lived to become very dear friends, and in her *Life
of Charlotte Brontë*, Mrs Gaskell has given the
world a most fascinating and vivid picture of the
tragic Brontë household.

The book brought her great fame, but it also
plunged her into trouble. The most serious came
from the managers of the Clergy Daughters' School
at Cowan Bridge where the Brontë sisters had been
starved and ill-treated, but the book strengthened
the growing conviction that the schools of England
were in need of reform. George Eliot wrote of the
book: "We thought it admirable, we cried over it,
felt better for it."

In all the work of Mrs Gaskell there is not one
ill-natured word, and she seemed to have the gift
of calling out the best in every one. "All of us,"
she once wrote, "have one look now and then,
called up on to our face by some loving thought,
and this, our highest on earth, will be our likeness
in heaven."

She died as she was quoting to her son-in-law

some words of his father—dead just a fortnight before. Had she finished the sentence she was uttering her next words would have been "When I am dead." But before she had reached them, she leaned forward and fell dead. She lies buried in the little chapel graveyard at Knutsford, which she has described to us in her novel *Ruth*.

For EU product safety concerns, contact us at Calle de José Abascal, 56–1°, 28003 Madrid, Spain or eugpsr@cambridge.org.

www.ingramcontent.com/pod-product-compliance
Ingram Content Group UK Ltd.
Pitfield, Milton Keynes, MK11 3LW, UK
UKHW012334130625
459647UK00009B/281